Fans

Compilation:

A. F. Tcherviakov (Introduction, text, catalogue, notes),
and with the collaboration of E. I. Moïsseienko,
T. K. Strijenova, L. A. Iakovleva

All photographs by:
N. N. Alexeiev, S. A. Petrov

Except: All rights reserved: p.18, 20, 22, 81, 86, 101, 118,
121, 139, 141, 148, 153, 184, 185, 187, 188, 189

Publishing Director: Paul André
Text: Alexander F. Tcherviakov
Translated from the French by: Brock Austrums
Layout: Parkstone Press
Typesetting: Russell Stretten Consultancy
Assistant: Céline Gallot

Printed and Bound in Europe
ISBN 1 85995 365 4

© Parkstone Press, Bournemouth, England, 1998

Fans

From the 18th to the Beginning of the 20th Century

Alexandre F. Tcherviakov

Collection of the Palace of Ostankino in Moscow

PARKSTONE PRESS

« Iskoustvo »

This album is the first in a series of publications dedicated to museum collections, concentrated today in the former palaces of the Moscow region. These collections consist of remarkable works of art, acquired by the former owners of these palaces, as well as works brought together much later.

In one of these former noble residences, Ostankino, constructed at the end of the 18th century for the Cheremetiev family, today is found an important collection consisting of figurative and decorative works of art. The collection of fans located there deserves particular attention. It was collected there relatively recently, mostly through donations. Currently, it consists of more than two hundred Russian and European masterpieces. It is mostly made up of gifts from collectors and of purchases from individuals.

I dedicate this album to the memory of my mother, Nadejda Alexeievna Tcherviakova (Boulyguina).

Pages 4, 10 and 11
1. Back of a two-sided fan:
"The Triumph of Amphitrite"
France. Around 1860.

"The fan is a device permitting one to fan oneself.
It is composed of a sheet of varied decoration, which one
unfolds and flutters."

I. N. Berezine.

Russian Encyclopedia Dictionary

"Several sticks or pieces of bone joined by taffeta or by a
picture glued on them, . . . The weaker sex has also attributed
to these sticks the function of a machine to create wind."

The Satirical Journal

2. Fireplace screen.
Russia. End of 18th century –
beginning of the 19th century.

CONTENTS

A few words on fans by Karl Lagerfeld

Let's not analyze the bibliography of written works on them or their history.

For me it is above all a useful, pretty, even beautiful object and can be the masterpiece of a great craftsman or a great artist.

The fan is from that family of objects which protect us, such as the parasol or the umbrella. In a large part of the world, men also carry them and have used them for millenniums. It is only in our regions, and particularly since the 19th century, that one has wished to make of them a weapon of femininity. In the language of the last century, it became the sword of the woman. One even used to say that it was the scepter of the world of a beautiful woman . . . (and the others, the less beautiful . . . ?) It was grotesque and exaggerated.

Men still carried them in the 18th century. It had the same role as the hand muff in the winter for both sexes.

If I lived in a cold country, I would wear a muff like the men of the Ancien Régime.

The fan and the muff are complementary. They keep the hands occupied and calm in the game of gesticulation.

A fan has spirit. There are so many ways to make use of it without needing to speak its famous language, which, in any case, is no longer understood. It has a heavy literary past and appears in famous works of painting throughout the ages. The fan wishes to be the screen of modesty. It prefers paradox to the cold dilemma of logic.

The Academy, in defining it, speaks of the "little piece of equipment which serves as a fan or as a portable screen." That gives weight to an object so light.

I hate that some call it a fly-chaser as they do in the Indies.

Let's forget the analytical and picturesque side of this object which I adore and which will not leave my thoughts.

As in the Egyptian cosmology, I see there the emblem of happiness and even a certain restfulness.

I dedicate the fan to Aeolus, the god of the winds.

I prefer it in folded paper. The feathers and the myrtle branches and locust of antiquity hardly aspire to modern life, where it plays the role of portable "air conditioning." It chases smoke away and protects you from bad breath.

Ronsard has already spoken of "Fans of the Air."

Unfortunately the fan craftsmen – I ought to say artists – are more and more rare.

In the middle of the 18th century, Paris alone counted more than 150 "master fan makers."

The Fan was the object of famous riddles. One of the most well known began:

"My body is but composed of long bones,
And I had all the time but skin on the bones,
I shine in company, and without any rest,
In the height of the summer, I am at all the parties."

This is how I will end my little preface

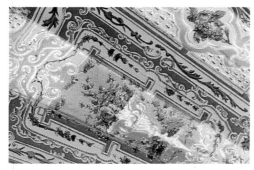

The Language of the Fan in the 18th Century

To yawn behind one's fan: *Go away, you bore me.*

To lift the fan towards the right shoulder: *I hate you.*

To lower the closed fan towards the floor: *I scorn you, I despise you.*

To lightly touch the closed fan to one's right eye: *When shall I see you?*

To signal towards oneself with the fan closed: *I always want to be with you.*

To threaten with the fan closed: *Do not be too bold, audacious.*

To raise the fan with the right hand: *Are you faithful to me?*

To hide the eyes behind one's fan: *I love you.*

To offer a fan: *You please me very much.*

To conceal one's left ear with the closed fan: *Do not disclose our secret.*

To hold the fan over one's heart: *I am yours for life.*

To slowly close one's fan: *I agree completely, I accept all that you say.*

V. Pokrovski. "Elegance in the Satirical Literature of the 18th Century." Moscow, 1903, p. 43

The Language of the Fan in the 19th Century

To completely open one's fan: *I am thinking it over.*

To place one's hand over the heart while holding the fan open in front of the eyes: *I love you.*

To indicate the floor near oneself with the fan: *Come close to me.*

To press the open fan with both hands against one's breast while slowly lifting the eyes: *I humbly request forgiveness.*

To lightly touch one's mouth repeatedly with the closed fan: *Could I speak with you in private?*

To completely open one's fan and wave it in the direction of one's interlocutor: *I would hope to always be with you.*

To look at one's closed fan: *I think of you all the time.*

To hold lightly with the left hand the closed fan over one's heart: *Are you faithful to me?*

The number of unopened blades indicate the time of a rendezvous: *At the agreed hour.*

To turn the inside face of the fan towards one's interlocutor: *I shall not be able to come.*

To move the end of the fan on the palm of one's hand, as if writing a letter: *I will let you know by mail.*

To wave away one's interlocutor with the closed fan: *I do not like you.*

To direct the open fan towards the floor: *I despise you.*

To open and close the fan repeatedly: *You are too bold, audacious.*

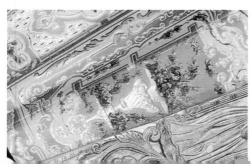

To angrily close the fan and turn it feverishly in one's hand: *I am angry with you.*

To press one's chin against the closed fan: *I am sulking.*

To write with the finger on the outside of the fan: *Let me know by mail.*

To look at one's open fan while rocking the head from side to side: *You do not want to know me at all.*

To turn with the right hand the end of the closed fan held in the left hand: *You are being deceived.*

To hold the two ends of the closed fan between the palms: *I require an answer.*

To indicate a seat with the fan closed: *Sit next to me.*

To indicate a seat with the fan open: *That's enough! You are boring me.*

To point several times to one's forehead with the fan closed: *Are you mad?*

To press one's chin on the open fan: *Stop your repugnant pleasantries.*

To press the closed fan against one's right shoulder: *I detest you.*

To repeatedly drop the closed fan half open into the left hand: *Not another word.*

To flutter the open fan towards oneself: *Dance with me.*

To cover the palm of the left hand with the open fan held in the right hand: *Keep it secret.*

To give the closed fan to one's interlocutor: *You please me very much.*

To place the open fan against the right cheek: *Yes.*

To place the open fan against the left cheek: *No.*

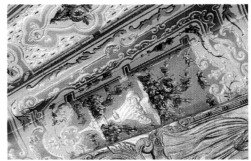

To place the closed fan against the right ear: *I'm listening to you.*

To hold the closed fan to the right temple: *Stop being jealous.*

To gracefully open and close one's fan: *Your desires shall be fulfilled.*

To lay the closed fan in the fold of the left hand: *I do not understand you.*

To gracefully hold out the open fan to one's interlocutor: *Welcome.*

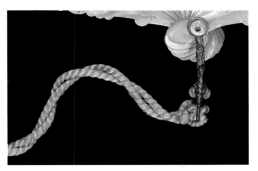

To impatiently pass the closed fan from one hand to the other: *I am very worried.*

While holding the open fan with the right hand to make it turn with the left hand: *My parents do not wish it.*

To tap with the closed fan between the fingers of the left hand: *We must interrupt our conversation.*

To press the closed fan to one's heart while holding it with both hands: *Spare me this unbearable company.*

To hang the closed fan from the right hand: *Adieu, good-bye.*

V. Pokrovski. "Elegance in the Satirical Literature of the 19th Century."
p. 44-46

11

*3. R. N. Nikitine.
Portrait of M. I.
Stroganova.
Oil on canvas.
Between 1721 and 1724.
Russian Museum.*

*4. Fashion engraving from
the journal, "Parisian
Fashions. Office of
Historic Fashions and
Costumes."
1746.*

There was a time when the fan, a little object now practically gone from our daily life, made up an integral part of the feminine costume and was very widespread in the life of the upper levels of Russian society.

Recently we have observed an increasing interest in diverse objects from the past which are today misunderstood or even lost. Fans fit in this category. But their value is not only in the fact that they are rare objects from life in bygone days. They deserve the most attentive observation and study as works of decorative art entirely in their own right, created and existing according to very precise rules of their own.

Unfortunately, until now, the collections of fans that are in the possession of museums, among which one often finds veritable masterpieces, have not been the object of any detailed study. They have not been recognized for their true value and their place in the national culture has not been defined.

Aside from several rare mentions in some articles or studies dedicated to costume art, journals have not

*6. Chiseled blades of a fan
with three cartels.*

*5. Fashion engraving from
the journal, "Parisian
Fashions. Office of Historic
Fashions and Costumes."
1777*

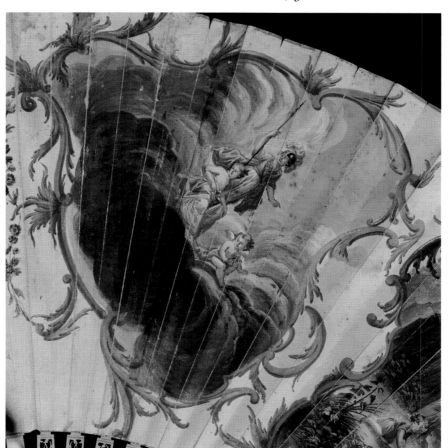

*7. Allegory of the Air.
Detail of the painting of a
sheet with three cartels.
Russia. Around 1750*

accorded a sufficient place to the works popularizing the history of fans in Russia.

Faced with this situation, the Palace of Ostankino, in Moscow, has time and time again been tempted to respond to the increasing interest in fans and to partially fill the void which has been left due to the absence of monographs concerning these objects. In recent years, exhibitions specially dedicated to the fan have been organized and some examples were displayed in exhibitions of various themes[1]. The publication of an album presenting certain fans from the 18th century was undertaken[2].

The present work can also be considered as the publication of the essentials of the collection, a first attempt, following the example of the collection of Ostankino, to present the history of fans in Russia from the 18th century to the beginning of the 20th century.

The fan collection of the Palace of Ostankino was assembled during a relatively short period. In 1956, the museum counted only eight examples. A generous gift from F. E. Vichnevski, famous Moscow collector, founder of the V. A. Tropinine Museum in Moscow, has represented a considerable contribution[3]. In 1956, the Palace of Ostankino was the setting for an exhibition of fans from his private collection[4] and two years later he gave to the museum all fifty works which had been displayed. This is how the collection of fans was born, which was subsequently dynamically completed. The pieces which followed were fans from private collections, fans belonging to individuals, donations from other museums, from antique shops, etc. . .

Some of the 18th century fans (catalogue #'s 22, 23, 25, 26) having belonged to the family of the painter V. P. Cheremetiev, a direct descendant of the Count N. P. Cheremetiev[5], founder of the Palace of Ostankino, represented a very valuable contribution to the museum collection.

8. Anonymous.
Portrait of a lady in a blue dress.
Around 1770.
Palace of Ostankino in Moscow.

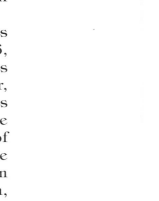

10. *Fashion engraving from the journal "Parisian Fashions. Office of Historic Fashions and Costumes."*
1788.

11. *I. P. Argounov.*
Portrait of V. A. Cheremetieva.
Around 1760.
Palace of Ostankino in Moscow.

9. *Fan with three cartels: "Knight with a Lady in the Park."*
Russia. Around 1780

One of the 18th century fans acquired by the museum is particularly remarkable (#31). It is one which comes from the collection of a famous scholar, a specialist in the history of fabric and fashion, the great connoisseur of fans L. I. Iakounina, who has assembled an interesting

collection of decorative works of art consisting of nearly one hundred examples[6].

E. V. Goldinger, talented painter and keen connoisseur of paintings, gave to the museum an invaluable fan (#20), providing a great contribution to the development of the museums of Ostankino and Kouskovo[7]. In 1981, the Museum of Ostankino acquired several fans from the Museum of Porcelain at the Kouskovo castle from the 18th century, which had obtained them from the private collection of the famous Muscovite L. I. Rouzskaïa.

In 1992, the collection of the Museum of Ostankino assembled two hundred fans from the 18th century to the 20th century. This is one of the largest and most valuable collections of fans owned by a Russian museum. Its contents and diversity are not surpassed except for the collections of the Museum of Heritage and of the Museum of History[8].

The Ostankino collection allows for the evaluation of the great diversity of fans which existed in Russia and the study of the particularities of style, form and decoration of each period. Its value also resides in the fact that it is constituted primarily of fans made in the second half of the 18th century, that is to say, during the golden age of the fan.

However, in spite of the obvious importance of this collection, specialists have not given it nearly enough attention. A whole series of inexact dates and of approximate information on the origins of the fans bears witness to this. The motifs of the sheets have not all been analyzed, the symbolic representations are not always explained, the names of the creators do not always correspond to artists who really existed. Through a detailed study of the collection, the origins of certain fans were clarified and reassigned. The contents and significance of certain examples were explained. In certain cases, the author was identified and information was obtained concerning the authors of some rare sheets which still bear their signatures. This work has permitted the establishment of the true value of each individual object, and of the value of the collection in its entirety and to explain in a more detailed manner the role and significance of the fan in society life.

It is useful at this point to say a few words on the denomination of the subject of our study. In Russian,

12. Fashion engraving from the journal: "Der Bazar, illustrierte Damen-Zeitung." 1888.

13. Fan with three cartels: "The Rendezvous." France. Around 1780.

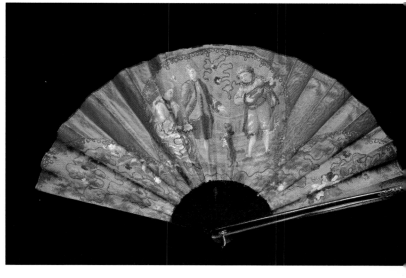

14. Stage fan of the actrice of the Marie Theater in St. Petersburg, N. V. Petrova. Russia. Around 1910. Palace of Ostankino in Moscow.

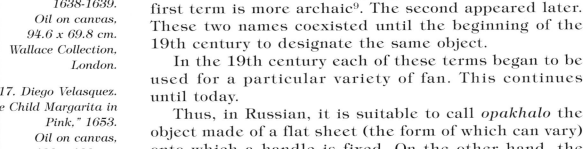

16. Diego Velasquez. "Woman with a Fan," 1638-1639. Oil on canvas, 94.6 x 69.8 cm. Wallace Collection, London.

17. Diego Velasquez. "The Child Margarita in Pink," 1653. Oil on canvas, 128 x 100 cm. Kunsthistorisches Museum, Vienna.

there exist two synonyms to designate two distinct varieties of this accessory: *opakhalo* and *veier*. The first term is more archaic[9]. The second appeared later. These two names coexisted until the beginning of the 19th century to designate the same object.

In the 19th century each of these terms began to be used for a particular variety of fan. This continues until today.

Thus, in Russian, it is suitable to call *opakhalo* the object made of a flat sheet (the form of which can vary) onto which a handle is fixed. On the other hand, the accessory made of several blades glued one on the other (which form the body of the fan: its frame), joined together at their inferior ends by a rivet and at their superior end, which flares out, either by a ribbon or by a wide band, is called *veier*. In this variety, upon folding, the blades of the fan take on a compact form, enveloped on each side by panaches, rigid blades.

It is necessary to note that only the Russian language employs the two terms opakhalo and veier to differentiate these objects, distinguished by their form. The other European languages designate these two varieties by the same word: *l'éventail* in French, *der Fächer* in German, *fan* in English, *el abanico* in Spanish, *il vantaglio* in Italian, etc. . . To make the difference between the two varieties clear, these languages can use description of different traits of

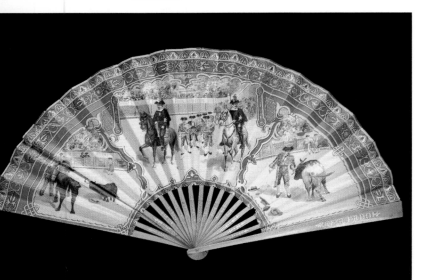

15. Souvenir fan: "The Bullfight." Spain. 1910's. Palace of Ostankino in Moscow.

each. In English, for example, the word opakhalo designates a fan with a handle, or a screen, and the term *veier*, a folded fan.

The history of the fan has its roots deep in antiquity. In the beginning, this accessory served as protection from the sun, to refresh and to swat away annoying insects. The first prototypes that we know of today were probably gifts of nature: a branch, a large leaf, a tuft of feathers. Numerous legends and myths from diverse cultures and countries all claim to be the first witness to the distant origin of the fan. However, we can probably consider a medieval European legend as the one describing the most distant epoch of the birth of the fan. This story recounts how our grandmother Eve, bothered by the attentive gaze of Adam, once awakened, pulled down the branch of a tree and began to fan herself all the while contemplating with curiosity the marvels

18. *Anthony Van Dyck.*
Portrait of a young woman
with a child
(portrait assumed to be
Balthasarine Van Linnik
and her son), around 1618.
Oil on wood, 131 x 102 cm.
Hermitage Museum, St.
Petersburg.

Page to the Right:

19. Detail
Fan with three cartels:
"Rural Scene."
England. Around 1790.

Top
20. Antoine Van Dyck.
Portrait of Maria Raet, Wife
of Philippe le Roy, 1631.
Oil on canvas,
215 x 123 cm.
Walace Collection, London.

Bottom
21. Antoine Van Dyck.
Marie-Louise de Tassis,
1629.
Oil on canvas, 129 x 93 cm.
Collection of the Princess of
Liechtenstein, Château
Vaduz.

22. Antoine Van Dyck.
A Genoese Woman,
1621-1623.
Oil on canvas,
200 x 116 cm.
Gemäldegalerie, Berlin.

of Eden[10].

Our epoch has conserved from antiquity some of these written accounts just as some images confirm the usage of fans among different cultures. For the Chinese poets, the screen fan appeared in their country near the beginning of the second millennium before Jesus Christ. As for the folded fan, it appeared in China during the tenth century before Jesus Christ. It seems very likely that it came from Japan[11].

One finds references to the fan in the epic Indian narratives such as the Mahabharata and the Ramayana[12].

For the people of ancient Egypt, the fan was the symbol of happiness, of celestial calm and was the sign of great merit[13]. This is why fans with long handles can be seen on the frescoes and papyrus sheets representing victorious processions and ceremonies, as for example the case of the fresco mural from the 17th century before Jesus Christ, found in the Berlin Museum which represents a pharaoh's procession[14].

Fans were equally widespread across the Aegean Sea, as seen in a number of representations on antique vases and ceramic statuettes similar to the ancient Greek figurine of Tanagra dating from the 4th century before Jesus Christ, made in baked clay ("The Woman with the Fan") from the collection of the Berlin Museum[15].

In Rome as well, where they were called *flabellum,* the fan was an indispensable accessory to women's fashion. The most prized fans were those in peacock feathers, very expensive and imported mainly from the island of Samos[16].

It is interesting to note that near the end of the Roman epoch and the beginning of the Byzantine (3rd – 5th centuries after Jesus Christ), fans returned to the form of small flags fixed to a short shaft[17].

For the first Christians, fans were also indispensable everyday objects. They were used in sickrooms as well as in ceremonies in the churches. Originally their use corresponded to their first function: they were used to cool off and to swat away insects from the ritual wine and bread. Eventually they became an integral part of the ritual; they took on a symbolic meaning during the liturgy, then, having acquired a particular form, they were called ripostes[18].

We have little information on the usage of fans in high society of the beginning of the Middle Ages. This is explained perhaps by a religious interdiction and by the difficult living conditions of the period. But, according to certain researchers, the fan had not completely

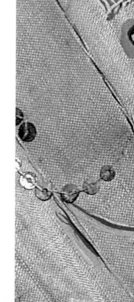

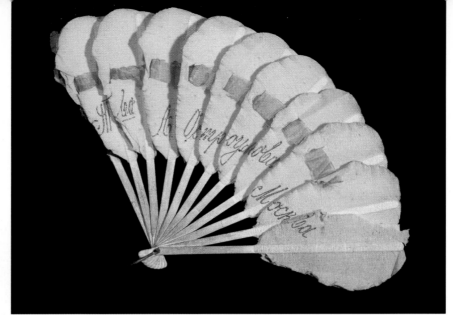

23. Souvenir fan from the store of the A. V. Ostrooumov Company in Moscow.
Collection of the Author.

24. Antoine Van Dyck. Portrait of Isabella Brant, around 1621. Oil on canvas, 153 x 120 cm. National Gallery of Art, Washington DC.

Page to the right
26. Fan with sequins. Russia. Beginning of the 20th century.
Glasses in shell, gloves in leather, handbag decorated with grains of glass, theatre program.

27. Antoine Van Dyck. The Marquise Balbi, end of 1621 – beginning of 1622. Oil on canvas, 183 x 122 cm. National Gallery of Art, Washington DC.

disappeared. References to the subject are found around the time of Queen Théodelinde (6th century), in the abbey of Tournus (9th century) and in other places[19]. We think that this accessory spread throughout the entire world from the 11th century[20]. But this probably meant screens, and in Europe, they were most often made with the feathers of ostriches, crows, peacocks and less often with other materials[21].

In France fans carried, until the 16th century, the name fly-chasers, which recalls one of the original functions of swatting away insects[22]. It was not until the 16th century that the term éventail or fan entered into the language[23]. According to most researchers, it is during this period that the folded fan appeared in Europe, which seems to have been introduced on the continent at the end of the 15th century – beginning of the 16th century. From China, it was exported to Portugal and Spain and then made its appearance in other

25. K.E. Makovski. Portrait of a young woman in a sable cape, beginning of the 20th century. Oil painting. Collection of the author.

Following pages:

28. Fan in ornamental motifs. England. End of the 18th century.

29. Francisco de Goya. Marquise of Santa Cruz, 1797-1798. Oil on canvas, 142 x 97 cm. Musée du Louvre

countries[24]. During this period it was above all the aristocracy of the greatest courts who used it. For example, Catherine de Médicis contributed to its adoption by the French court. King Henry III himself was taken by a passion for fans, which never ceased to amaze the courtesans[25].

It is during the 17th century that folded fans began to become the most widespread. But during this period screens were used as well. This coexistence of two related forms can be observed in numerous examples,

which are reflected in figurative art. Thus, a portrait in the art gallery of Devonshire shows us Queen Elizabeth holding in her hand a screen made of feathers[26]. From the same period, a fashion engraving from Augsbourg, dated 1629, shows women equipped with two kinds of

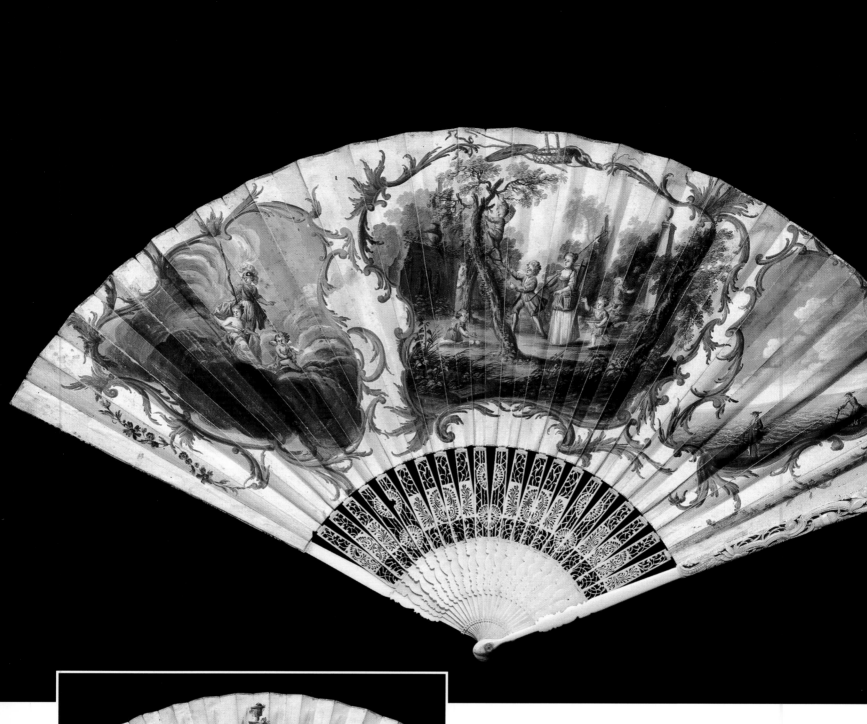

30. *Two-sided fan with three painted cartels.*
Russia. Around 1750.

31. *Back of the fan.*

fans[27]. A little later, in the album of Vincel Hollar from the years 1643-1645, "Spring, Summer, Autumn, Winter," several feminine figures dressed in period costume are also shown with both types of fan[28]. And even the rare form of a flag fixed to a shaft continued to exist until the end of the 17th century[29].

In the middle of the 17th century, the folded fan had definitely supplanted the screen. If those imported from Asia are excluded, the principle manufacturers were the English, who produced inexpensive models, and the Italians, who specialized in more costly painted fans. But soon the predominant place of fan production, as in fashion and art in general, became France.

Near the end of the 17th century the demand for fans increased and the development of their production necessitated the founding in France of a special corporation of master fan makers[30]. In the 1770's, the city of Paris alone counted 150 fan workshops with 6,000 workers[31].

In the case of Russia, information concerning fans is very poor and does not provide a true idea: of the origins of their appearance, of the level of their production, of the nature of their sale or of the scope of their popularity, nor the names of the master fan makers. This is what is remarked upon by the rare Russian authors who more or less explained the history of the fan[32].

The first documents which confirm the use of fans

32. Detail
Two-sided fan with three painted cartels.

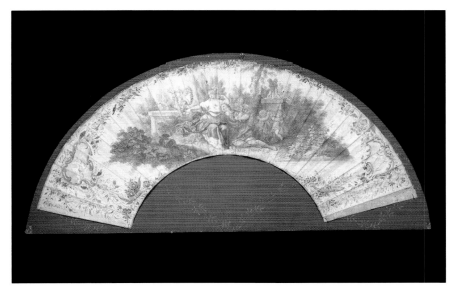

33. Two-sided sheet of the fan:
"Renaud and Armidia."
Russia. Middle of the 18th century.

in Russia, particularly in the Imperial family and their court, date from the 17th century. Therefore, we can assume that screens had already been introduced into Russia around this time. For example, Sophie Paléologue could well have brought some from Italy to Moscow, among other objects in current usage. All the more so since in the middle of the 15th century, fans were very widespread in Italy. But this is only speculation as no

27

documents can confirm it.

Information we do have at our disposal shows that in the 17th century, in Russia, there coexisted the two types of fans: screens, most often made of ostrich feathers, and folded fans, in satin or parchment.

Thus, the Czar Michel Feodorovitch possessed: " . . . a screen in wood, adorned with gilt and in diverse colors, the handle[33] wrapped with crimson fabric (1629); a round Turkish screen, in white feathers, crimson and black, with a mirror in the centre, the handle in Indian wood; a folded fan in parchment, decorated in diverse colors, with a wooden handle (1634)"[34].

Aside from the screens coming from Asia, this is the first mention of folded fans, visibly the western model, the sheet of parchment of which is painted and fixed on a wooden frame.

35. Two-sided fan with five cartels: "Rebecca at the Well." Russia. Around 1780.

34. Two-sided fan with three cartels: "The Rendezvous in the Park." 1770's.

The links established in the 17th century with the countries of Western Europe became closer and closer. There were, in the Imperial family, just as in their court, influential people who had assimilated certain aspects of European morals and who, in spite of Russian traditions, preferred European costume and other imported items. One can cite as an example a parent of a Czar, the boyard N. I. Romanov[35]. The future field marshal of the St. Petersburg region, B. P. Cheremetiev himself, began to follow European fashion at the end of the 17th century[36].

The infatuation with items from Europe probably also established itself with the progressive adoption of fans of the two types by courtesans of Russian society. It is difficult to say to what degree their usage became widespread, if they were everyday accessories or only party finery. Nevertheless, in taking into account the specificity of fashion during this period, it can be assumed that the fan was not very standard and that it was not used except in particular cases; during ceremonies, for example.

It was especially before Peter the Great that screens in ostrich and peacock feathers with richly decorated handles could be seen. The most expensive pieces were, of course, destined for the Czarinas.

"March 13 of the year 137 (1629), the servant Vassili Ivanovitch Strechnev brought to the palace of the

36. Fan with three cartels: "Knight with Lady in the Park." Russia. Around 1780.

37. *Fireplace screen.*
Russia.
End of the 18th century –
beginning of the 19th century.

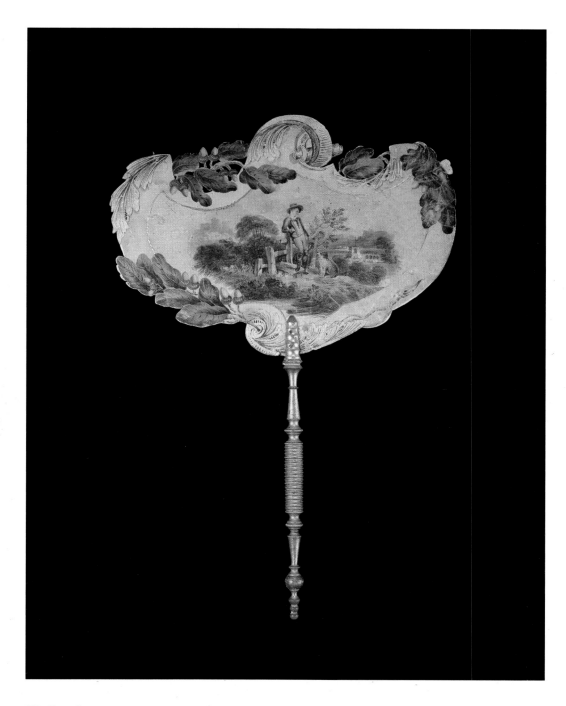

38. *Fireplace screen.*
Russia. End of the 18th
century – beginning of the
19th century.

Czarina Eudoxie Loukianovna a fan of ostrich feathers with a jasper handle of engraved gold, the gold blades were embedded into the end of the handle, between which were set flashes of rubies and emeralds, and near the jasper ornament and the small neck were set little crimson rubies and emeralds, above the neck and on the back, pieces of pearls; on the other side of the fan, on the neck was set a jasper stone in which flakes of gold were inlaid, including crimson rubies. In the middle of the neck, a cut crimson ruby with small emeralds on the sides; next to the jasper stone and the small throat of the neck, on the back, was a pearl; the case for the fan had a coating of solid gold, it was a Turkish piece[37]."

In Russia, as in other countries, fans of the two types, similar to this description, were often diplomatic gifts sent by directors or clergymen to important people[38].

According to the inventory of the palace treasury, dated 1640, in 1630, the Czar Michel Feodorovitch received as a gift "a fan of black feathers with a jasper handle, with a gold frame in which were inlaid small crimson stones, rubies and sapphires. Its case in fine crimson Moroccan leather. It cost 56 roubles and 12 kopecks. It was sent as a gift to the sovereign by the Patriarch Cyril of Tsaregrad and by the Archemandrite Philophéi in the year RPM"[39].

In 1632, "the metropolitan Guennadi de Kafim sent the sovereign, with the clerk Davyd, a feather fan, with a carved wooden handle, carrying in the centre a mirror with a cover. The end of the handle was bone and the mirror was framed by red feathers. Its price was 60 roubles"[40].

The inventory of the treasury of the Czarevitch Alexis Mikhaïlovitch reported in 1638, "a feather fan. The handle is set with a turquoise stone, in which blades of gold are inlaid, and in the gold are small crimson stones and flashes of rubies, emeralds and turquoise. The feathers are framed on both sides with circles of

39. Sheet of the two-sided fan: "Games in the Park." France. Middle of the 18th century.

jasper. In each jasper stone and in each gold inlay are seven crimson stones. In the circles of jasper, on one side a crimson stone is inlaid in gold, surrounded by eight green emeralds, forming a square and on the other side, a large crimson stone set in gold. Above each circle is a triangular emerald. The fan is accompanied by a case. It is worth 44 roubles and 54 kopecks. It was offered to the sovereign Czarevitchby the Patriarch of Tsaregrad Cyril and the Archimandrate Amphilokhi in the year 140"[41].

Fans were much prized in the court and it is not by chance that they were inventoried in so much detail in the palace inventories. They were appreciated and were left as legacies just as with other precious objects.

In this way the fan mentioned above, given by the metropolite de Kafim, Guennadi, to the Czar Michel Feodorovitch was next recorded in the inventory of the treasury of Czarina Eudoxie Loukianovna, and later in 1649 it figured among the objects used by the Czarina Irina Mikhaïlovna[42].

As to the fan given in 1630 by the Patriarch Cyril, it was given that same year by the Czar to his son Alexis, and after the death of Czar Michaïl Feodorovitch, the new Czar Alexis Mikhaïlovitch gave it to the Czarina Natalia Kirillovna[43].

The passing on of this fan from one person to another is at least as interesting as the appraisal inventory minutely describing each of its details[44].

As one sees in the conserved documents, in the court fans, were not only popular with women but just as popular with men. But it could be that men used them only on ceremonial occasions.

In 1671, during a procession from the village of Preobrajenski, fans were given to the Czarevitches Feodor and Ivan. "June 2 of the year 179, taken from the arms room, among the gifts of this year 179, two fans of crimson satin, were given to the palace of

Following pages:

40. Two-sided fan representing a pastoral scene.
France.
Around 1760.
And details.

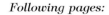

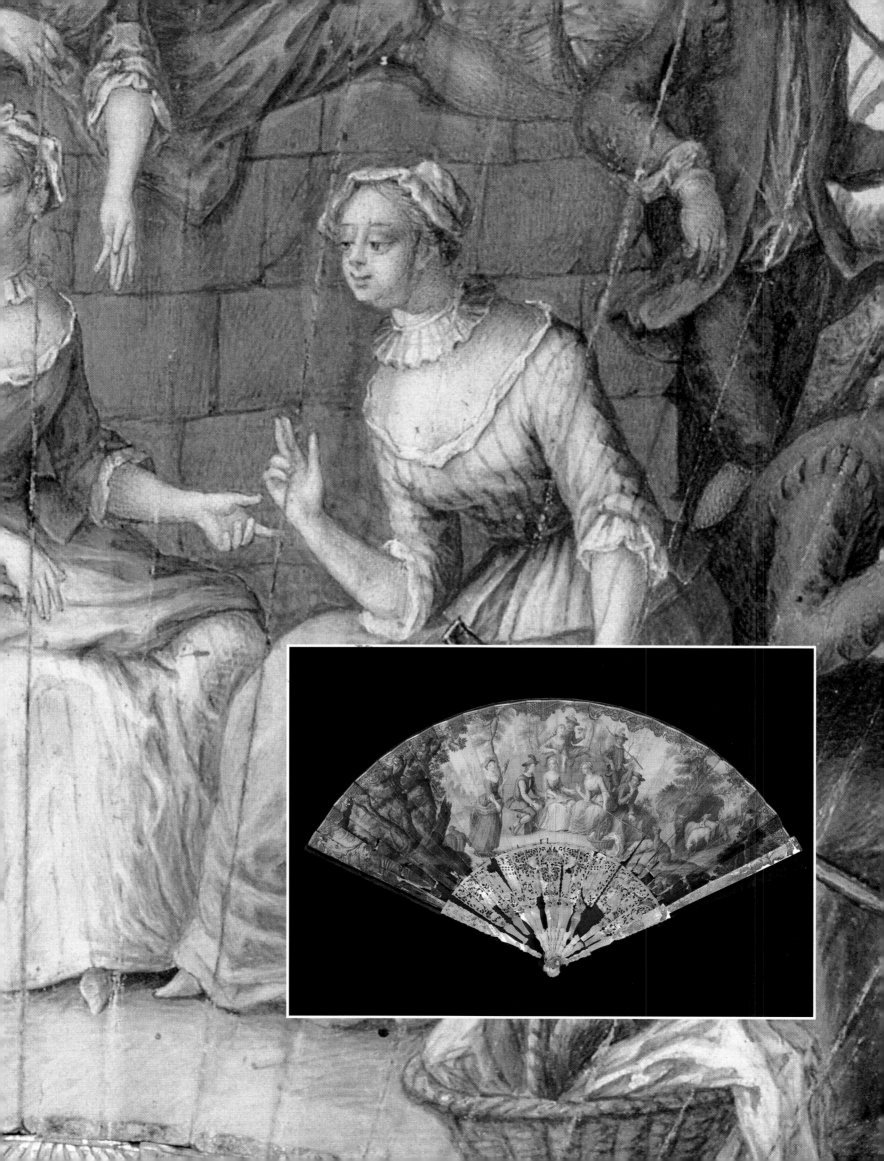

his highness the sovereign, during the procession of Preobrajenski. The boyard and armorer B. M. Khitrovo took these fans and gave them to the palace, to Czarevitch Feodor Alexeievitch as well as to Czarevitch Ioanne Alexeievitch"[45].

Among the objects confiscated from the confident of the Czarina Sophie, the disposed prince Vassili Golitsyne, figured a modest "fan of vermilion satin, with a wooden handle"[46], of a value estimated at only 30 kopecks.

In the inventory of goods made at the time of the insurrection of boyard Feodor Leontievitch Chaklovityi, supporter and close friend of Sophie Alexeievna, executed October 11, 1689, is "a fan of German feathers, colored, the wooden handle of which is painted and holds a mirror and is surrounded by embroidery and silver from the mirror. Its value is 50 kopecks"[47].

In the second half of the 17th century, the great popularity of fans among the court permitted the organization of their production in armory workshops. We know that on special invitation in these shops, famous bone sculptors from Kholmogore,

Belarus, Poland worked, as well as artists specializing in other areas[48]; there is no doubt that they participated not only in the creation of fan frames but on the entire object as well.

It is believed that in the armory, fans were usually made of sheets of satin (in fabric). The artisans often gave their works to the Czar and members of his family, generally on the occasion of Easter[49].

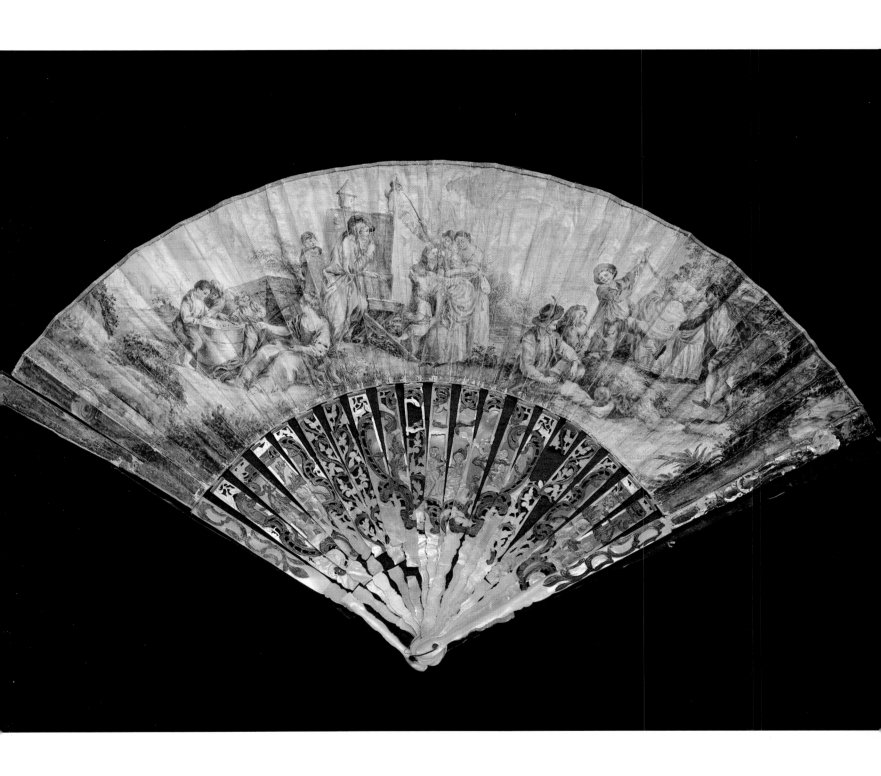

*41. Two-sided fan representing a scene of a
rural festival.
France. Around 1760.*

42. *Two-sided fan:*
"The Birth of Venus."
France. Around 1760.

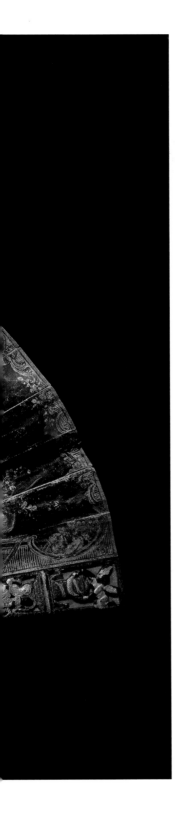

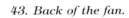

"In 1686 four fans in satin were made for the Czarevenas, of which two were crimson, two yellow of a smaller size, which required 14 archines of satin, 14 sheets of Alexander paper and 8 pounds of German cyprus wood"[50]. The fans previously mentioned, given to the Czarevitches Feodor and Ivan, during the procession of Preobrajenski, are also among these presents.

The documents of the palace inform us of another use of fans in daily life. In this usage, it can be assumed that the members of the court imitated the Imperial family. Thus, some fans were bought at low prices in the markets of Moscow, or specially made in the workshops of the armory, with the purpose of being used in the palace baths.

"April 11 of the year 178 (1670), for the bathroom of the great sovereign, two paper fans valuing 20 kopecks were purchased. April 19 of the year 178, for the bathroom of the great sovereign, small stones for a fan and a crimson ribbon of two archines were purchased"[51].

We have the happy surprise to discover in the inventories of the palace a piece of information very valuable to our study; the name of an artist who produced fans in the armory workshop.

"Year 183. Eftiféï Kouzovlev decorated all the gifts of the armory given to the court this year 183 (1675) (. . .) : two peacock feather fans, two crimson satin fans . . ."[52].

We can have an idea of the kinds of fans used, during the period which we are describing, thanks to a Dutch specimen in mica, dating from the border between the 17th and 18th centuries, which is found today in the collection of the Museum of Ostankino (#64). This fan was created in the exotic style, called the style of the East Indies. On the sheet of transparent mica, two half-naked female figures are drawn surrounded by greenery. The edges of the sheet are bordered by a fringe made of silk thread of diverse colors, which seem to imitate bird feathers. The exotic form of the fan, the sheet of which recalls that of a tropical tree, is accentuated by the curved handle, wrapped tightly with a colored leather ribbon and partially gilded.

43. Back of the fan.

At the beginning of the 18th century, the reforms of Peter the Great broke with the old way of life, completely disrupting the customs of Russian society. After the charter of 1718 on assemblies, the women of the nobility began to take a larger part in the life of the court and to participate in various parties, receptions and ceremonies. Catherine I, who had a court on the western model, loved luxury and who, as written by one of her contemporaries, was herself "weak and magnificent in all senses of the word"[53], greatly contributed to these transformations.

44. Fan:
"Abigaïl facing David."
France. Around 1759.

Among numerous borrowings from the west, paralleling European fashion, the folding fan, which supplanted the screen before the reign of Peter the Great, was adopted by the nobility. Its entry into the life of the upper levels of Russian society under the reign of Peter I is confirmed in paintings (a portrait of M. I. Stroganova). The absence of direct information on the production of fans in Russia at the beginning of the 18th century, just as the documents confirm, do not allow us to picture how things happened during this period. Nevertheless, a certain number of measures taken by the government of Peter the Great contributed without a doubt to the development of this production.

Thus, from 1715 to 1722, first in St. Petersburg, then in other Russian cities, manufacturing organizations were created, in which regulation had a positive influence on relations between the different artists and consequently on the quality of fabrication of various objects, particularly fans, given that various specialists participated in their creation: bone sculptors, paper workers, painters, etc...[54]

Unfortunately, nearly none of the fans created in Russia during the first half of the 18th century remain. We know of two, specially created for the Empress Anna Ioannovna, painted by L. Tiorane. These are in The Hermitage Museum[55].

It is believed that the Russian fan "reigned" and developed considerably during the reign of Elizabeth Petrovna[56].

40

45. Fan:
"Bird Catchers in Love."
France. Around 1770.

46. Two-sided fan:
"Pastoral."
France. 1770-1780.

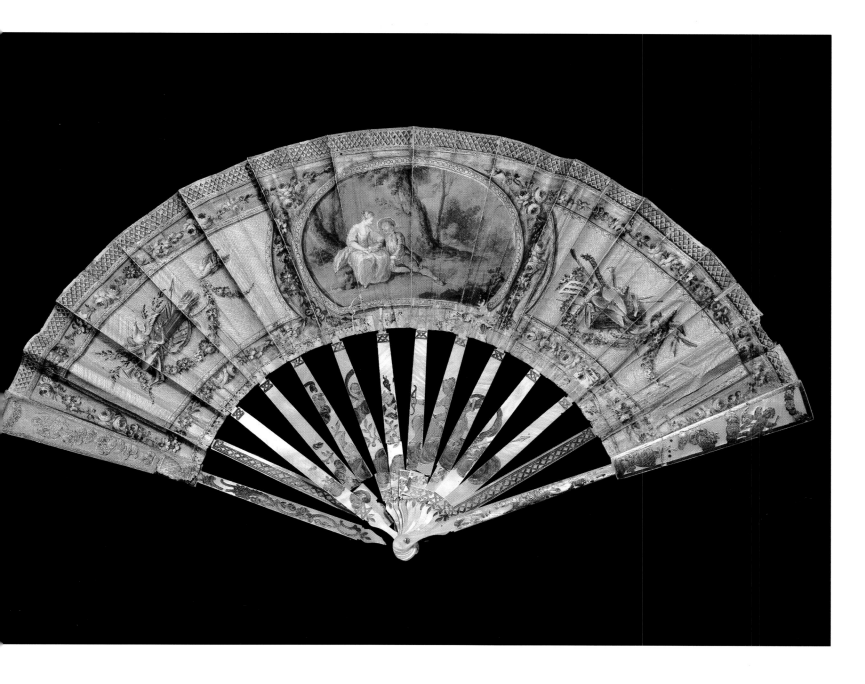

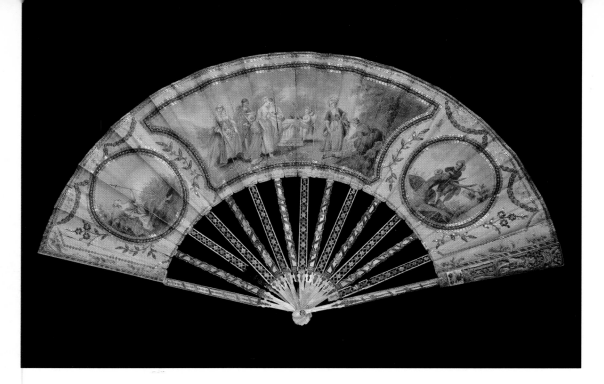

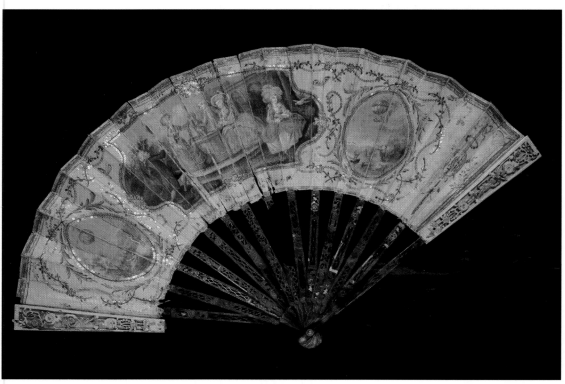

Preceding pages:

47. Fan:
"Family Love."
France. 1770-1780.

48. Two-sided fan:
"The Altar of Love."
France. 1770-1780.

49. Fan with three painted cartels.
1770-1780.

50. Fan representing a group of
musicians.
France. Around 1780.

During this period a change can be seen in the themes used in the decoration of fans. The apotheosis of severe and pompous subjects gave way to mythological images exalting the beauty of the Empress and the influence of her court[57]. The frames became lighter and more gracious. The blades, formerly tightly stitched together and lacking in decoration were now open and finely engraved.

In The Hermitage Museum, a rare signed fan, the subject of which is taken from mythology, can be seen. It was painted by Vassili Nikanov and the fan itself was created by the fan maker Andréï Morozov. It represents an extremely rare case among Russian fans, in which the creator is identified. This same fan maker is also mentioned in the account books of the palace and in books on the subject of fan production[58].

A fan from the collection of Ostankino (#1) dates from the same period. It is made up of three cartels and represents the three elements. The craftsmanship and style of the elegant engraving of the superior edges of the blades and the rocaille elements of the panaches and the use of ivory (or of mammoth?) (from which the frame is made) permit it to be counted among the best work of Russian bone sculptors, perhaps from Kholmogore, who were working in the capital. The sheet

51. Fan with three cartels: "The Rendezvous." France. Around 1780.

of this fan was certainly painted under the influence of the symbolic and allegorical themes that were very widespread in the art of the period. In Russia, after the publication in 1705 of the book "Symbols and Emblems," the representation of symbolic images was particularly popular. The creator of this fan did not escape this influence. On the paper sheet, three cartels surrounded by rocaille scrolls in motifs of vegetation represent three personifications of the three elements:

Air, Earth, Water. The left cartel presents Air, the heavens as well as the symbol of all that is celestial, divine. This representation is in part confirmed by the allegorical figures of Minerva, Juno and Zephyrus, seated on clouds. Minerva (goddess of war, of science, of art and wisdom), is close to Juno (goddess of kingdoms and empires), queen of all the gods. And Zephyrus is also seen, the personification of air itself[59].

The central cartel represents Earth in the usual fashion, in the form of a scene from daily life; impish children plucking an apple tree.

The element Water, on the right cartel, is represented in the form of an expanse of sea without end, which makes an allusion to infinity and thought, and the figures, standing on the shore, symbolize meditative contemplation.

This fan is a work of the first order of decorative art from its period. The talented collaboration of painters and bone sculptors permitted a harmonious union and expressive manner of ornamental and figurative motifs

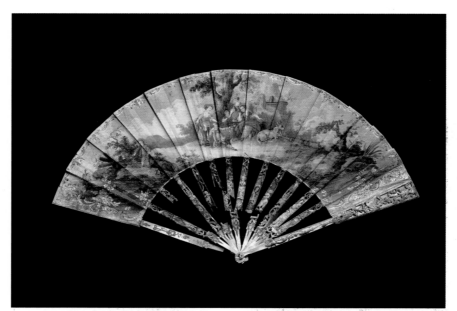

52. Two-sided fan representing a pastoral scene. France. Around 1770.

in applying them to the particularities of the form of the object and in bringing out most clearly the characteristic traits of baroque art: the abundance of decoration, the magnificence of composition.

In the accounts of the court office dating from June 1734, interesting evidence of the enlargement of the degree of utilization of fans in Russia is found. Among other acquisitions for an Italian acting troupe, there is a mention of the payment of the following purchase: "for the comedy on the monkey, the fan and two pairs of gloves; one rouble and 80 kopecks"[60]

In Russia, as well as in the other countries of Europe, the veritable golden age of the fan began in

Page to the right:

53. Two-sided fan with five cartels: "What Did the Knight Say?" France. Around 1780.

the middle of the 18th century. It is particularly characteristic of the reign of Catherine II. The folded fan became an obligatory accessory and was an integral part of women's fashion. No woman dared to be seen in public without a fan. In the hands of its owner, the fan seemed to become an active detail, a participant of sorts in the general theatrics which accompanied luxurious ceremonies, parties and balls.

As an Englishman wrote of it, "the fan was an item so widespread that a woman without a fan felt just as ill at ease as a knight without a sword"[61].

During this period the demand for fans became very great and did not cease to grow. A considerable number of these objects were imported from various countries in Europe. The collection of the Museum of Ostankino displays fans of the 18th century exported from: France, Germany, England, Italy, and Holland into Russia. Some bear witness to former commercial relations in the form of customs stamps and seals of commercial organizations. Thus, the custom stamp of the port of St. Petersburg in the form of an eagle with two heads and the inscription SPB Port. Tamoj (customs port of St. Petersburg) is affixed on the back of the French fan "The Birth of Venus" (#11). One can also see stamps of this type on the German fans "The Rendezvous" (#36) and "Gallant Scenes" (#35), as well as on the fan representing parrots surrounded by flowers (#41).

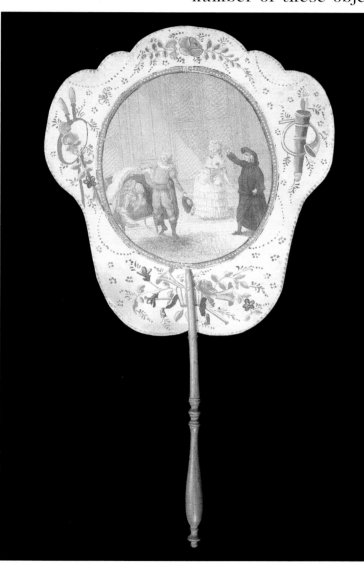

These stamps are particularly valuable when they are accompanied by a date, which permits a more precise establishment of the date of fabrication of the fan. For example, the customs stamp of St. Petersburg and the number 1761 are printed on a German fan representing a pastoral scene (#29). The customs port of Revel stamped its mark in 1791 on a fan imported from England, on which appears a "Rural Scene" (#48).

Due to the import of western fans, branches of foreign

55. Back of the fan: "The Marriage of Figaro."

56. Theatre screen: "The Marriage of Figaro." France. End of the 18th century.

Page to the left:

54. Theatre screen: "Blaise and Babette." France. End of the 18th Century.

companies were created in the capitals, in which merchants worked, and where they conducted their commerce in fans. The newspapers of the capital spoke of them incessantly:

"In the fifth line across from the Academy of Art, Yohann Hamm sells haberdashery items such as: women's finery, straw hats, scarves and embroidered shawls, muslin, women's coats and cotton dressing gowns, gloves, fans, etc."[62]

"A person possessing a shop on the Kouznetski Bridge, in the house of fabrication of Simoni cards, has brought back to Saint Petersburg new merchandise such as: perfumes (. . .), fans of all types and latest fashions, the best tobacco, feathers for women in the new fashion (. . .)"[63].

"In the house of Beckett, near the Kouznetski Bridge, Benners purchases solitaires for women, repeating watches, fans in the new style (. . .). All of these are sold at a very modest price"[64]. Five days later the owner indicated the price "very modest" of a fan: "from 25 roubles to 150 kopecks each"[65].

There were certainly commercial enterprises owned by Russians but we have not been able to find any direct evidence. But this suspicion is strengthened by a commercial stamp on the German fan "Family Scene" (#39): "1789. Chelkotov. Moscow". Under this inscription can be seen another, which is barely readable: "1789. Bou ... lek. T.V".

Along with the import of fans from western Europe, we observe their arrival from Asia. The public announcements in the newspapers of the capital bear witness to this, as, for example, in "Moskovskie Vedomosti" ("The Moscow Bulletin").

"In the rows of silverware of the shop #120, Chinese fans of various types are sold, in silk as well as in paper"[66].

"In the middle of the rows of vegetables, in shop #21, we have received new model Chinese fans in ivory and rattan, in taffeta and paper, the most beautifully painted in the world, in various colors, which are sold by the shopkeeper Timophéï Zlobine"[67].

However, it is necessary to note that despite the craze for the Chinese and Japanese styles and themes, which manifested themselves in the decorative art of the period, Russia received fewer fans from Asia than from western Europe. This can be explained by ethnic considerations and by the moral and religious standards

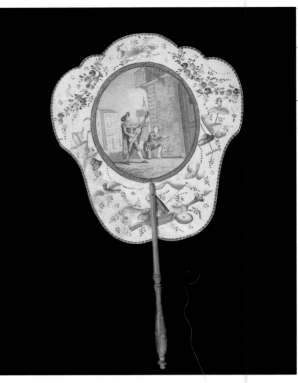

58. Theatre fan: "Tartuffe." France. End of the 18th century.

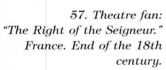

57. Theatre fan: "The Right of the Seigneur." France. End of the 18th century.

Page to the right:

59. Theatre fan: "The Barber of Seville." France. And detail.

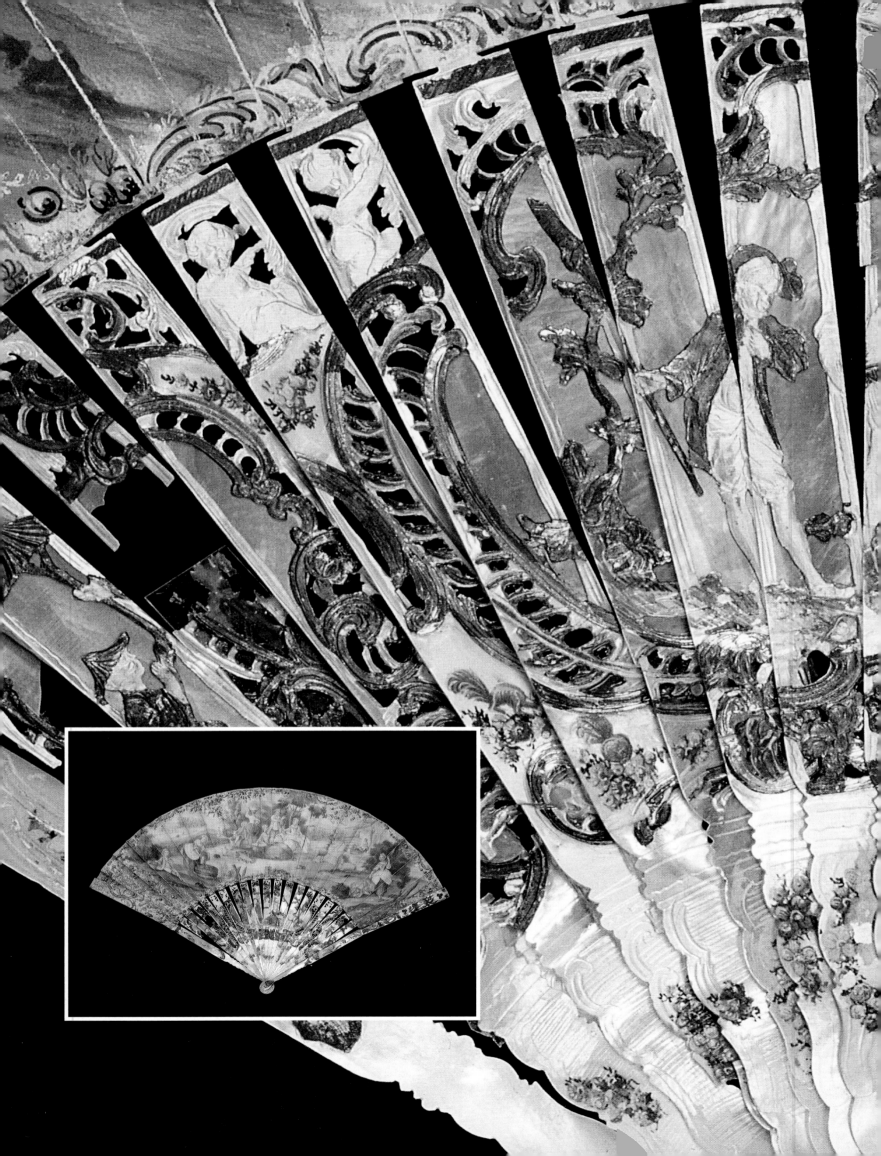

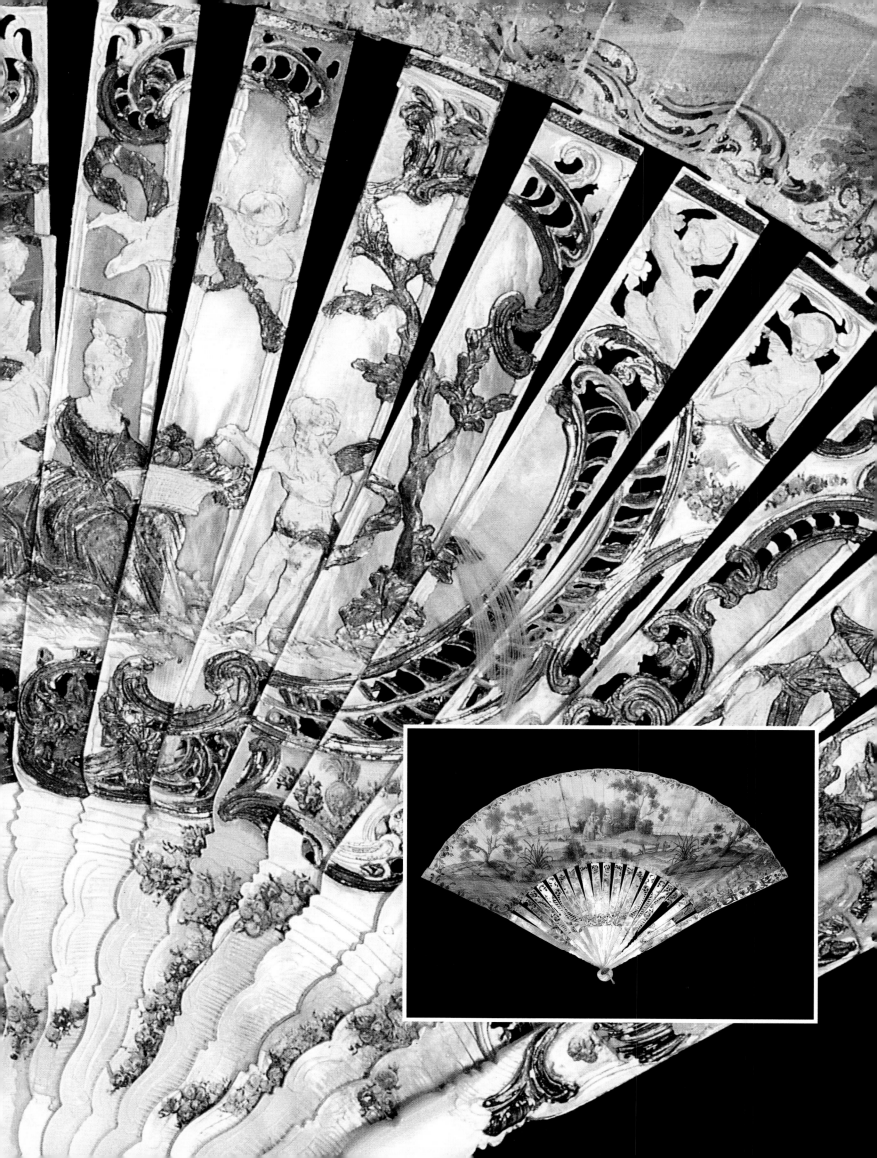

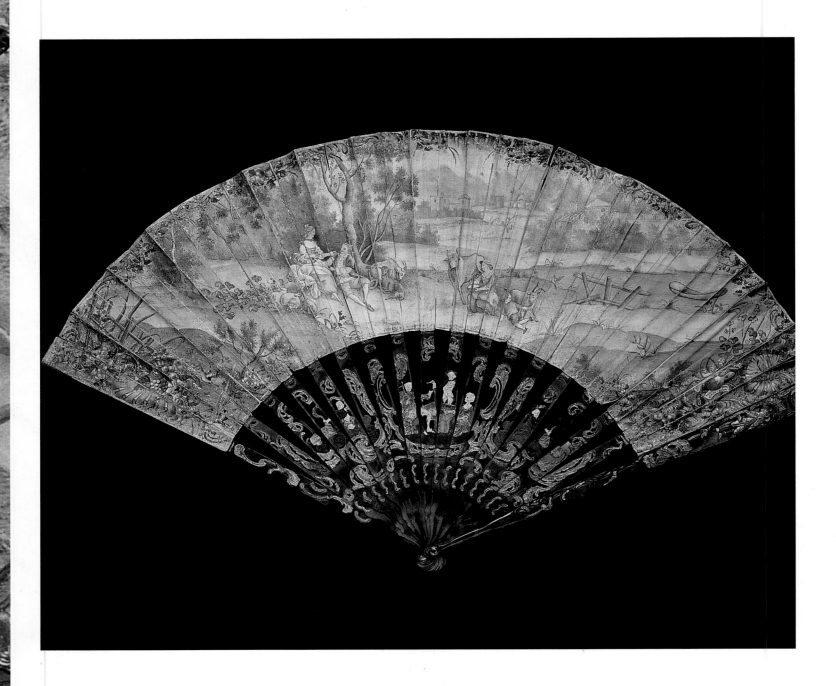

Preceding pages:

60. Two-sided fan:
"The Wine Harvest."
Germany. Middle of the 18th century.

61. Back of the fan.

62. Fan representing a pastoral scene.
Germany. Around 1760.

Page to the right:

63. Two-sided fan representing a pastoral scene.
Germany. Around 1760.

which were held by the ladies of Russian society. This is why Asiatic fans which found purchasers (fairly rare) were probably of neutral motifs, representations of plants, animals or birds.

The strong demand for fans not only increased their foreign importation but also contributed to the development of their production in Russia.

In the capitals, in St. Petersburg or in Moscow, fabrication workshops and fan repair shops were created. As a general rule, their owners were artists of foreign origin[68]. This fact is also confirmed in the public announcements of the newspapers of the capitals.

"Pierre Schindler, who makes fans of the very latest style and repairs old ones, lives between the 2nd and the 3rd Mechanskaya on the Catherine Canal, in the Menchikov house, at number 394"[69].

The following year, in the newspaper "Sankt-Peterbourgskie Vedomosti" ("The St. Petersburg Bulletin") there appeared a new advertisement from the same artist:

"Pierre Schindler makes different fans of the very latest fashions and repairs old ones with great know-how. He lives on Sadovaïa Street, in the Neimann house, at number 815"[70].

A little later the same newspaper published:

"The mechanic Spiegel creates objects of carved art in mother-of-pearl and in ivory, such as chessboards, candle screens, fans, etc. He also repairs old fans and applies taffeta to them. He lives on the Catherine Canal between the 2nd and 3rd Mechanskaïa, in the house of the merchant Menchikov, at number 129"[71].

In Moscow, if one believes the advertisements published by the "Moscow Bulletin," a certain Isaac Zouderban owned a fan workshop. He possessed his own letterpress, in which he printed the sheets of the fans.

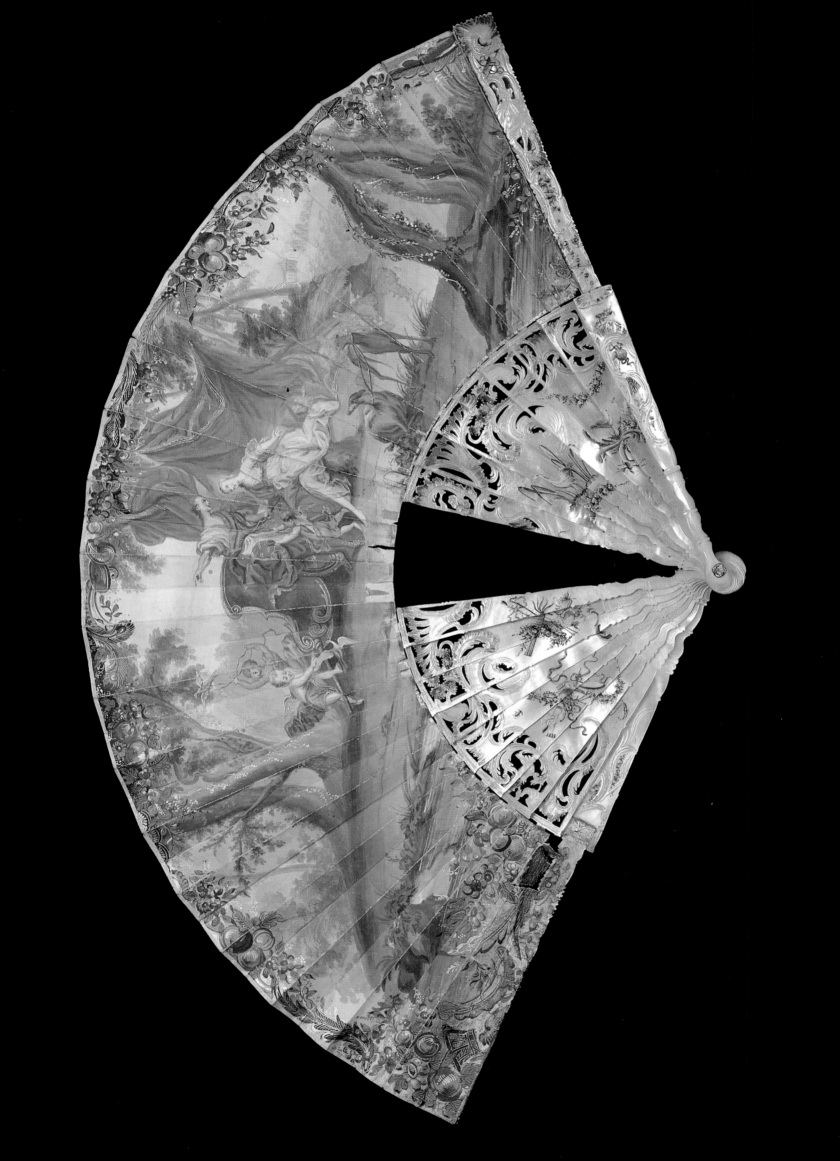

66. Two-sided fan:
"The Toilette of Diane."
Germany. Around 1760.

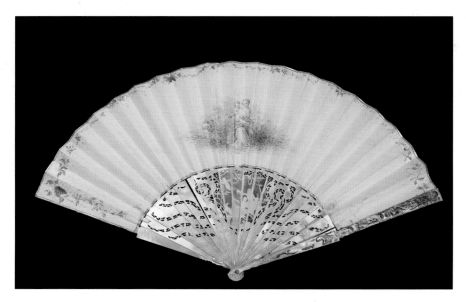

67. Back of the fan.

68. Two-sided fan representing
allegorical scenes.
Germany. 1760's.

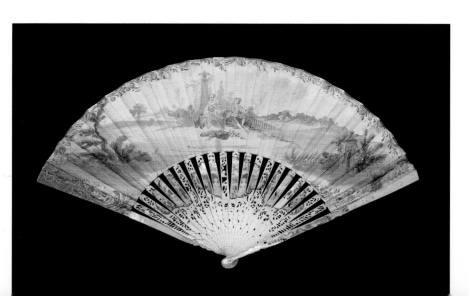

69 Back of the fan.

"In the first part, in the parish of St. Nicholas the Maker of Miracles Mokryi to Zariadie, in the house of the owner of the letterpress Isaac Zouderban, at number 101, we sell: paper for fans of various designs, costing 25 to 100 kopecks, as well as mounted fans. Those who own old fans can bring them to have applied new paper with a design. Also, those who wish to sell their fans can find here an agreeable price[72]. Here are sold not only colored fan paper, but we also embroider fans with gold taffeta; we also sell all kinds of bones for fans"[73].

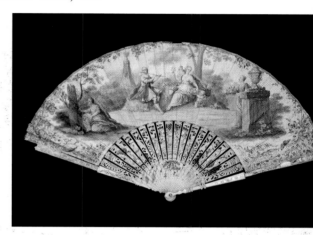

Information concerning the price of a fan in the shop of this same Zouderban is also very interesting: "We sell newly printed fans some of which are carved, in particular:

1) Fans representing various portraits and carrying inscriptions: (Minerva visiting the Muses): 3 roubles;
2) (Homages to Armor) consisting of 41 figures: 2 roubles and 50 kopecks;
3) The Boston Game: 2 roubles and 50 kopecks;
4) Imports: 3 roubles each;
5) Assorted Chinese fans: 2 roubles each"[74].

*70. Two-sided fan:
"Two Lovers."
Germany. Around 1760.*

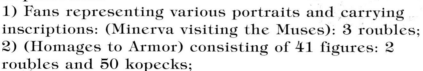
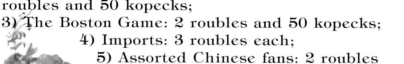

But alongside such fan workshops, the owners of which were foreigners established in Russia, Russian workshops and even factories specializing in the production of fans were created.

Thus, in 1750 in Moscow, a fan factory was created which was owned by Vladimir Roussinov "and associates." It was registered with the Chamber of Commerce and its owner regularly gave accounts of its activity in sending reports to the Chamber of Commerce, which provides knowledge not only of the address of the factory but also the height of its production.

"The bulletin of the fan factory of Vladimir Roussinov and Associates, which is located behind the gates of Mesnitski in the City of Earth, in the parish of the church of Saint Nicholas the Maker of Miracles Derbinski, in our own house, that is to say in the five apartments"[75].

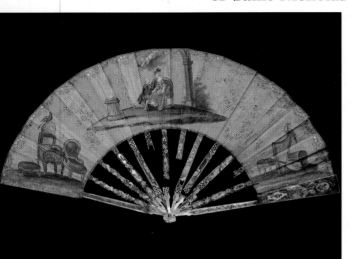

71. Fan:
"The Rendezvous."
Germany.
1770-1780

In 1752, "up to 10 people of both sexes worked in the factory to fold the fans, wash the ivory, tint the paper. The reports enumerate the machines, the materials and the instruments used in the production of fans. Among them one can find a press, in which the sheets are printed from a copper plate, the colors of the paint and the various instruments for cutting ivory. This factory was valued at 1,700 roubles[76].

May 3, 1753 Roussinov's co-producers and co-owners were designated under the names of Pierre Filatov and the apprentice Andréï Filatov. And if, in 1752, three painters worked with the apprentice, there were henceforth four: Alexis Petrov, the son of Bachkyrov, Nikita Savinov, Semion Petrov, Pavel Matveïev. Six artists worked sculpting bone: Aphonassi Dmitriev, Grigori Ivanov, Andréï Emelianov, Feodor Vassiliev, Mikhaïlo Moïsseïev, Fadéï Dmitriev, who were "hired by the factory for a daily wage." In addition, there were "six women who [folded and glued] the sheets at their top end and [tinted] them. They were all engaged by the week and by the day"[77].

In 1751, the factory produced more than 85 dioujines of fans of all types for a total amount of 225 roubles and 80 kopecks[78]. In 1752, in six months, "up to 38 dioujines of fans of different sizes and prices were produced for a total of 133 roubles and 44 kopecks"[79]. In six months, in 1753, "18 dioujines were made, for a total of 139 roubles. All were sold"[80].

It is interesting to compare the prices of fans sold by the factory and those by the boutiques and shops (Zouderban and Benners for example). Six different fans were, in 1752, valued and sold at 6, 9, 15, 18, 20 and 68 kopecks each[81].

In 1754, the factory was directed by Ivan Erine and during the course of the first six months produced 42 dioujines of fans for a sum of 196 roubles and 48 kopecks. "And these fans were used in Moscow by people of diverse functions and all were sold"[82]. The factory prospered. Its production increased: "in 1758, 78 dioujines of fans at 360 roubles and 50 kopecks were produced. In 1759, 98 dioujines for a sum of 390 roubles. And the

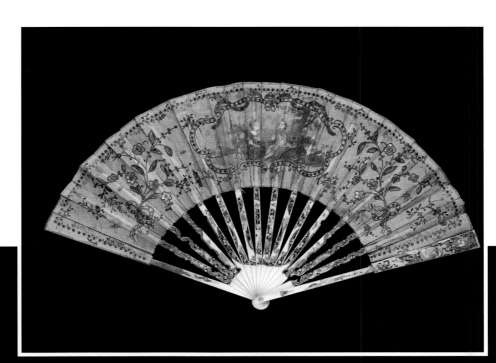

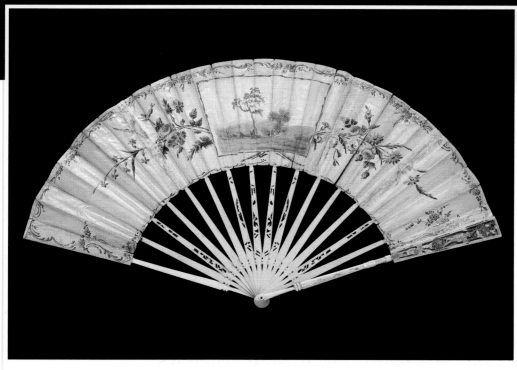

74. Two-sided fan:
"The Rendezvous."
Germany. 1770-1780.

75. Back of the fan.

factory was valued at 2,600 roubles"[83].

The associate of Roussinov, Pierre Filatov, seemed to separate himself from the business and created his own fan factory, with 29 workers, with a value of 2,500 roubles, in 1757[84]. That same year, various fans were manufactured for a sum of 561 roubles and 60 kopecks[85]. The composition of the workers in this factory is interesting: "1) 6 master craftsmen; 2) a freeman prints the sheets, assembles them, fixes them to the frame and does the gilding; 3) five women work the saw, make the assemblage and cut the bones; 4) five freemen, one of which a painter, comes from the Chancellery of State, with an individual treatment and, to which I teach the art of engraving; 5) five free painters"[86]. In 1765, this factory was already valued at 3,900 roubles and the level of production for six months, for the period of 1765 to 1768, represented from 33 to 61 dioujines of fans, for a total sum of 114 to 250 roubles[87].

The list of materials employed for the production gives an indication of the great diversity of fans sold by the factory. For the frames, wood, bone and mother-of-pearl were used. The sheets were made of paper with printed or drawn motifs. To decorate the blades and

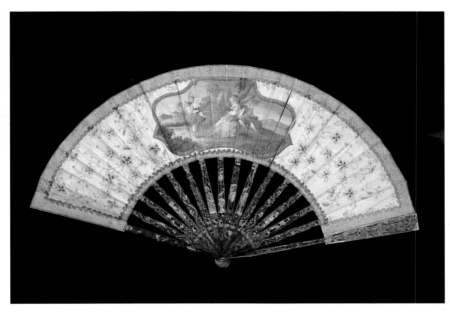

76. Two-sided fan representing a gallant scene. Germany. 1770-1780.

the sheets, various pieces of metal, gold leaf and solid gold were used[88].

The simple enumeration of the work the type of work done by the craftsmen who worked in the factories, provides evidence of the numerous operations required in the production of fans.

The Encyclopedia of Diderot and Alembert[89] furnishes

valuable information on the nature and order in which these operations were accomplished, with clear illustrations in support.

The most varied specialized craftsmen took part in fans' creation. Among them were: painters, engravers, jewel makers, sculptors of wood, bone and other materials, specialists in paper, fabric and embroidery.

In the 18th century, the blades of the frame were most often made of: ivory, shell, mother-of-pearl, and less often of wood, copper, gold and silver. Fans with magnificent sheets and the frames of which are made of cow or horse bone (called "animal bone") are also found. This considerably reduced the price. At the same time one could pass off "animal bone" as imported ivory. That is, for example, the case of the fan "Rebecca at the Well" (#5) which dates from the 1780's, the frame of which is "animal bone."

*77. Fan:
"Family Scene."
Germany. Around 1780.*

In Russia, for the manufacture of fans, abundant use was made of mammoth ivory, discovered during excavations in Siberia as well as walrus tooth, from which Russian bone sculptors created all sorts of objects.

In general, the blades of the frame were decorated with engravings, finely finished or in relief, often accentuated by painting, sculpting or inlaying. The protective blades, called panaches, were the most abundantly and richly decorated. The frames of the most expensive fans were adorned with colored enamel, set in bronze, gold or silver, and precious stones.

A German fan representing allegorical scenes (#33) provides a good example of a complex construction technique of blades, done with talent. In order to play with the light and make them shine, these blades, in bronze ornamented with openwork, are placed on a base of extremely thin mother-of-pearl, which shows through the openwork of the carving.

The shell blades of the Italian fan "Dawn" (#57), are heavily inlaid

Following pages:

*80. Two-sided fan with three cartels.
Germany. Around 1780.*

81. Back of the fan.

64

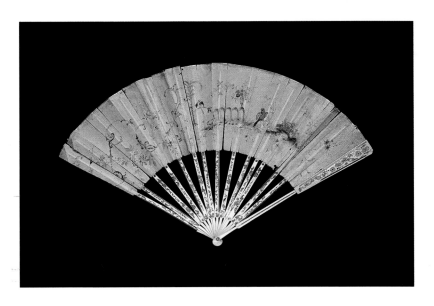

78. *Two-sided fan representing parrots surrounded by flowers. Germany. Around 1780*

79. *Two-sided fan: "Two Musicians." Germany. 1770-1780*

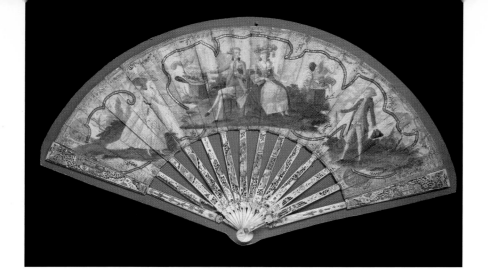

*82. Fan representing a gallant scene.
Germany (?). Around 1780.*

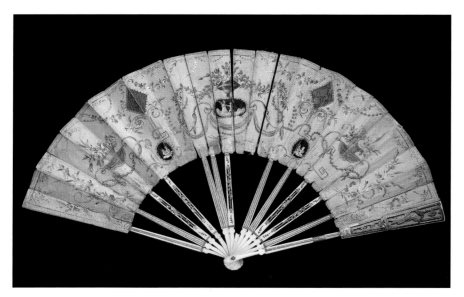

*83. Fan representing Love near
the altar.
Germany. 1780-1790*

*84. Two-sided fan:
"Distractions in the Park."
Germany. End of the 1790's.*

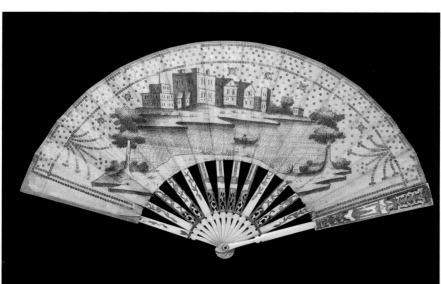

*85. Fan representing an urban
landscape with a river.
Germany. 1790's.*

with gold arabesques of a very fine design. The frame of the Russian fan with three cartels mentioned before (#1), which is older, is distinguished by the great artistry with which it was produced. To create a carving of such a high quality required master experimental carvers of bone, whose obligations and relationship to the work were determined by the thirty-nine paragraphs of The Instruction issued on August 24, 1727. Then, so that the masters as well as the carvers and lathe workers would always have it in mind, these regulations were annexed to the list of Russian workshops beginning in 1761[90]. The fifth paragraph of the Instruction stipulates

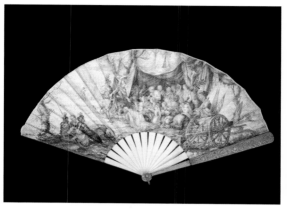

86. Fan:
"The Clemency of Alexander the Great."
Germany. (Poland ?). Middle of the 18th century.

that "each master must endeavor to execute his art to the best of his abilities, without asking who does what in the workshop, nor wonder about the salaries of others, as used to happen. If he earns little, he must not take the work of another master without declaring it. He must do good work for a good price, just as there must not be jealousy in this area. The masters must not suffer from contempt or nurture offenses from each other, and certainly, in their art, the masters must not dirty the reputation of others"[91].

In the "Artisan Charter" of 1785, the idea of the development of knowledge and the mastery of artisans working bone, shell and wood is expressed as well[92].

A decree in 1747 required that the finished products not be put up for sale in shops and stores until each was inspected. This is why the articles were periodically inspected in the stores. They would be seized and could not be sold if they were not made the object of a special authorization.

Indeed, on January 18, 1789, in the shop of the Italian Buzeta, non inspected merchandise was discovered, among which: "nine fans of carved bone, nine snuffboxes in wax, shell and bone covered with bronze and with chiseled mountings"[93].

In the 18th century, the folded sheet was fabricated from materials such as paper, silk, parchment, or skins. They were decorated with paintings, embroidery, an application of lace and other materials. In the 18th century, the painting was generally produced in gouache, less often in India ink, and sometimes it consisted of a representation

87. Fan:
"Dance with a Drum."
England.
Second half of the 1790's.

88. Fan with three cartels:
"Rural Scene."
England. Around 1790.

Page to the right:
89. Fan representing an
allegorical scene:
"The Young Girls and Love."
England. Around 1790.

90. Fan:
"The Coronation."
England.
Second half of the 1790's.

Following pages:

91. Fan with three cartels:
"Werther."
England. Around 1790.

92. Fan:
"Game of a Child."
England. Around 1790.

engraved on the paper or silk.

Near the end of the 18th century, an Englishman named John Robert Cousins discovered watercolor and developed this art. A secondary technique to begin with, it was progressively transformed into one of the principle methods and began to be employed in the painting of fans[94].

In the 18th century, the designs of fans were extremely varied and the richness of the motifs and the artistic processes and decorations were inexhaustible, as is seen in the collection of Ostankino.

The sheets were often decorated with compositions with several figures, the subjects of which were borrowed from mythology, Biblical legends, famous literary works and even historical events.

The sheet of the fan #2, the work of an anonymous Russian painter, represents a meeting scene in the magical gardens of Armidia between the legendary knight Renaud and the sorceress herself. It consists of the reproduction of an episode of a poem very popular in Russia in the 18th century, written in the 16th century

by the Italian poet Torquato Tasso, "Jerusalem Liberated." Chief of a detachment of Crusaders, under the influence of his love for the sorceress Armidia, Renaud forgets his duties as a soldier. It is this episode that the painter has reproduced. Having removed his armor and tenderly embraced his beloved, whose reflection Renaud admires in a mirror. The painter, obeying a figurative principle for achieving a decorative task, accomplished his task very well. The composition is adroitly inserted in the half circle of the sheet, uniting harmoniously with the landscape in the background and the decorative framing of vegetation and shell.

The painting of this sheet, done in the 18th century,

consists also of a narrative imagery specific to this period.

But in the fan "Rebecca at the Well" (#5), created in the 1780's, we see a new artistic approach. The motif is borrowed from the biblical story recounting how Abraham sent his loyal slave into the country of his birth, in Mesopotamia, to find a wife for his son Isaac. Near the well, in the city of Nahor, the slave finds what he is looking for in meeting the beautiful Rebecca[95].

In the design of this fan one no longer senses the intention to illustrate; to recount in pictures. A concrete motif is represented in a schematic fashion, in bending to the decorative objects of the whole, in a style purely decorative.

At the origin of the superb design of the French fan dating from the 1760's, "Abigail Facing David" (#12) is found the biblical tale on the legendary hero David. After his victory over Goliath, he became Emperor Saul's son-in-law. Later on the Emperor, suspecting that David wished to take power, planned to assassinate him. Having succeeded in escaping and rejoining a detachment in the mountains, David began to live the life of a bandit. One day he decided to punish Nabal, the rich tribal chief, for his refusal to furnish necessary supplies to the detachment. Ignoring the danger, Nabal dressed for a

feast. But his wife, Abigail, full of wisdom, reacted differently. After having assembled the supplies and presents, she went to meet David. David, touched by Abigail's gesture, renounced his intentions against Nabal. Upon learning what happened, Nabal became so angry that he fell sick and died. Shortly afterwards Abigail became David's wife[96].

The drawing of an English fan of the 1790's (#52), which was for a long time called "The Duo," was obviously crafted under the influence of the famous novel by Johann

Wolfgang Goethe, "The Sufferings of Young Werther." The heroes are reunited in a painted cartel (Werther writing his good-bye letter, Charlotte in despair and the child carrying a suicide pistol), which reproduces the tragic episodes of the novel.

The sheets of fans often reproduced famous paintings and fashionable engravings.

The sheet of a French fan (#15) is a miniaturized copy of the famous painting of Jean-Baptiste Greuze which the painter produced in 1763, "The Paralytic Served by His Children"[97]. And an Italian fan of the 1760's, executed with much art (#57) reproduced the subject of an immense fresco by the painter Guido Reni, "Dawn," of 1612-1614, in the Casino dell'Aurora (Palace Pallavicini-Rospigliosi) in Rome[98].

Many works were created in the favorite theme of the 18th century: the victories of Alexander the Great, picturesquely described by Plutarch. A painting having the same motif decorates a German fan (#47) made in the 1750's. Defeated and beating a retreat, Darius has abandoned his weapons, his chariot and his train with his harem. The victor, Alexander the Great, is shown among the prisoners promising them that they will keep their former honors and privileges. There is a painting on this theme in The Hermitage Museum[99]

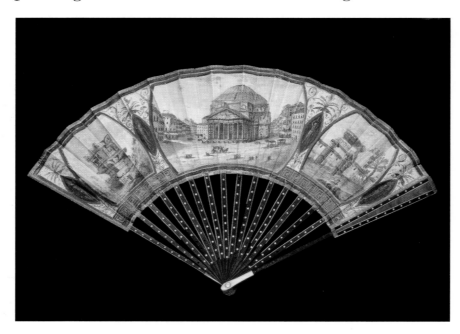

and at the Museum of Ostankino is found a magnificent engraving of very large dimensions created by Edelink[100]. In other respects Mazé-Sencier recalls in his book that at an auction taking place in Hamburg in the 1880's

*97. Two-sided fan:
"Dawn."
Italy. 1760's*

98. Back of the fan.

was a fan of Louis XV, "The Victory of Alexander"[101].

On one of the French fans, "What Did the Knight Say?" (#20), the motif of the painting is inspired by an engraving by N. Delaunay. Only the meaning of the representation of the fan differs a little from that of the original engraving in which one can see an Abbott in place of the knight. A woman is speaking to him while he is having his morning wash and studying a piece of cloth she is giving him.

The fans created especially for the rulers or for the nobles sometimes represented military victories, coronation ceremonies, or the portraits of their owners. That is, for example, the case of an Austrian fan from the second half of the 18th century which is found in The Hermitage Museum upon which is reproduced the apotheosis of the Empress Marie Therese. Also a Russian fan with two faces dating from 1750 and fixed on a gold frame, the sheet of which represents a procession of the Empress Elizabeth Petrovna and of the court of Tsarskoie Selo. The third fan of The Hermitage Museum reproduces the unfinished suburban residence of Catherine II, Pella, conceived by the architect Starov[102].

The characteristic infatuation of the 18th century for symbols and allegory is also noticeable in the drawings on fans. The symbolic images are not figured only separately but inscribed as well in the genre scenes or in the courtly scenes. Thus, on a German fan (#33) one can in some fashion follow all the events in the life of a human being, with his hopes and desires described in allegorical scenes. And Chronos (or Saturn), symbol of transience, contemplates the celestial, hidden behind a rock: "Do not vainly wait for this period to come again"[103].

The design of the German fan "Love Near the Altar" (#44) represents an allegory of devoted love and the readiness to sacrifice through two enflamed hearts on each side of the initial image which signifies, "they are two but no more than one"[104].

On the German fan "Family Scene" (#39) we see scenes in antique style of sacrificial flowers symbolizing admiration

99. Sheet of a fan painted in the style of Pompeii. Italy. 1780's.

100. Sheet of a fan representing a landscape with a waterfall. Italy. 1780's.

before the beauty of nature, the abundance and fertility of the Earth[105].

It is only natural that on objects such as these fans that the symbol which appears the most often in the most varied forms is that of love. Thus, on the sheet of the German fan "The Rendezvous" (#34), Cupid flies above the two lovers while holding a flaming torch, symbolizing never ending love[106].

The French fan "The Altar of Love" (#16) represents, among knights and ladies walking in a park, Love watching his victim near an altar. Some young ladies, having charmed Love and, as symbol of fidelity, two flying doves are represented on the English fan "The Young Girls and Love" (#49). One Italian fan, the design of which was created in the spirit of Pompeii frescoes, represents Love treading upon a book (knowledge) with his feet.

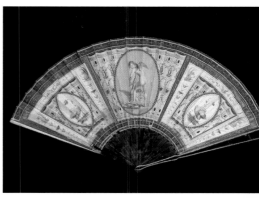

During all of the 18th century the designs having for a theme antique mythology, from where the motifs of Love were borrowed, were very popular.

In the collection of the Palace of Ostankino is a fan remarkable for its artistic qualities and for the dexterity of its execution, "The Birth of Venus" (#11), created in France in the 1760's. The painted part of the fan, which presents a composition of several characters and a decorative framing with expressive details, unites harmoniously at the blades of the frame and is executed with much talent. The blades are in shell cut in the form of columns and are fitted with openwork bars on which are applied ovals with gilded subjects in relief. The unity of the artistic construction and the manner in which the work was created betrays again the antecedents of the rococo period but one still notices the influence of a new style in the process of birth; classicism.

The German fans "Venus and Dawn" (#31) and "The Bath of Diana" (#32) are no less deserving of interest on the level of the virtuosity of their creation. These fans were also created around 1760. Although the design of the sheets also allows the perception of the visual narration specific to preceding fans, this one is subjected to the decorative

102. Sheet of the fan:
"The Ruins of the Antique
Temple."
Italy.
End of the 18th century.

project of the whole. It is also necessary to note the art of the engravers in the creation of the frame from a material as difficult to work as mother-of-pearl. Such work demands a very high level of skill on the part of the master engravers. The drawing of the English fan "Dance With a Drum" (#51) is equally inspired by antique images. Created at the end of the century, this object already bears witness to another decorative method, corresponding to the stylistic cannons of its period.

The imitation of Chinese models, in the manner called "chinoiserie," characteristic of the decorative art of the 18th century, often makes itself felt in the presentation of fans. Sometimes small Chinese figures are inlaid in the carving of the blades, as in the example of the German fan "The Wine Harvest" (#27) where gold blades in various colors in the style "chinoiserie" present abundant drawings, as on the German fan "Couple in Love With Lovers" (#41). Such is the painting of one of the Dutch fans (#65). Despite the European interpretation of the motif, the design is inspired and executed under the strong influence of the decoration of objects of applied Chinese art.

But the most appreciated subjects and the most widespread in the design of fans of the 18th century were scenes of gallantry, of love meetings, of pastoral and sentimental episodes. There were numerous variants in

80

103. Sheet of the fan:
"The Ruins of the Antique
Circus."
Italy. End of the 18th Century

Russian fans as well as fans from western Europe. The subjects were inexhaustible and were executed with a never ending whimsy. One can get an idea of this from two Russian fans created with great elegance: "The Rendezvous in the Park" (#3) and "The Knight and the Lady in the Park" (#4); from the French examples "Games in the Park" (#8), the fan representing a pastoral scene (#9), "The Rendezvous" (#19); and from the German fans "Gallant Scenes" (#36), "The Rendezvous" (#36), "The Two Musicians" (#40) and from numerous others.

It often happened that in these representations of a light genre, in these scenes of nonchalance, remarks on everyday life would be implied, sketches of everyday life. This is, for example, the case of a French fan representing a rural scene with dancing couples and spectators contemplating with interest the performance of a theater of strolling marionettes (#10).

On this level, the German fan "The Wine Harvest" is of great interest. It reproduces on one side a mundane society dressed for relaxation, a scene of grape harvesting and grape crushing and to the right, a woman spinning yarn with a spinning wheel (#27).

One can also see such scenes on two German fans, on which are represented simple villagers strolling on a path (#29) or a peasant tending cows with a small

Following pages:

104. Fan in mica representing two female figures.
Holland (Colony of Indochina ?). End of the 17h century – beginning of the 18h century.

105. Kitagawa Utamaro Portrait of Ohisa of the tea shop of Takashimaya, 1792-1793.
Xylograph in color with a background in mica, 376 x 247 mm.
Collection of R. N. Shaw.

106. Fan in mica.
End of the 17th century – beginning of the 18th century.
Chandelier and books.
Holland. 17th century.

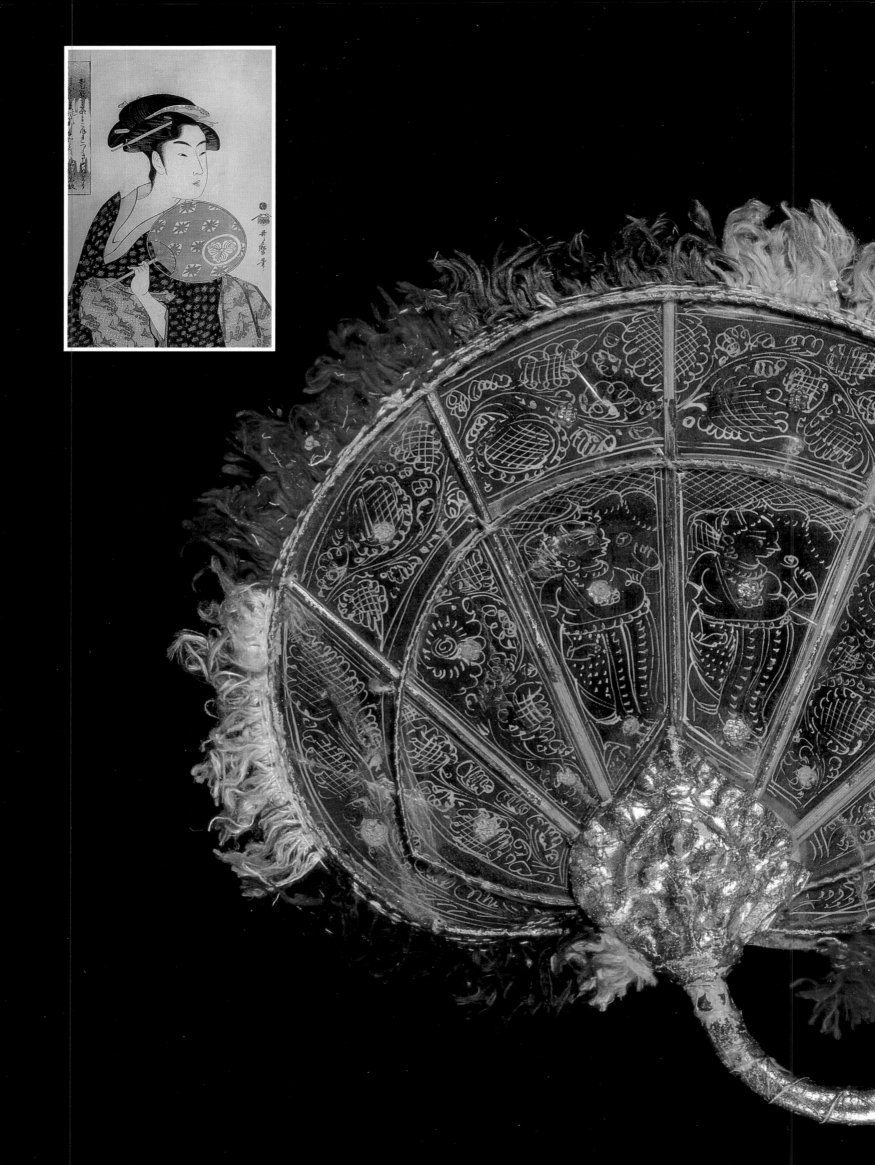

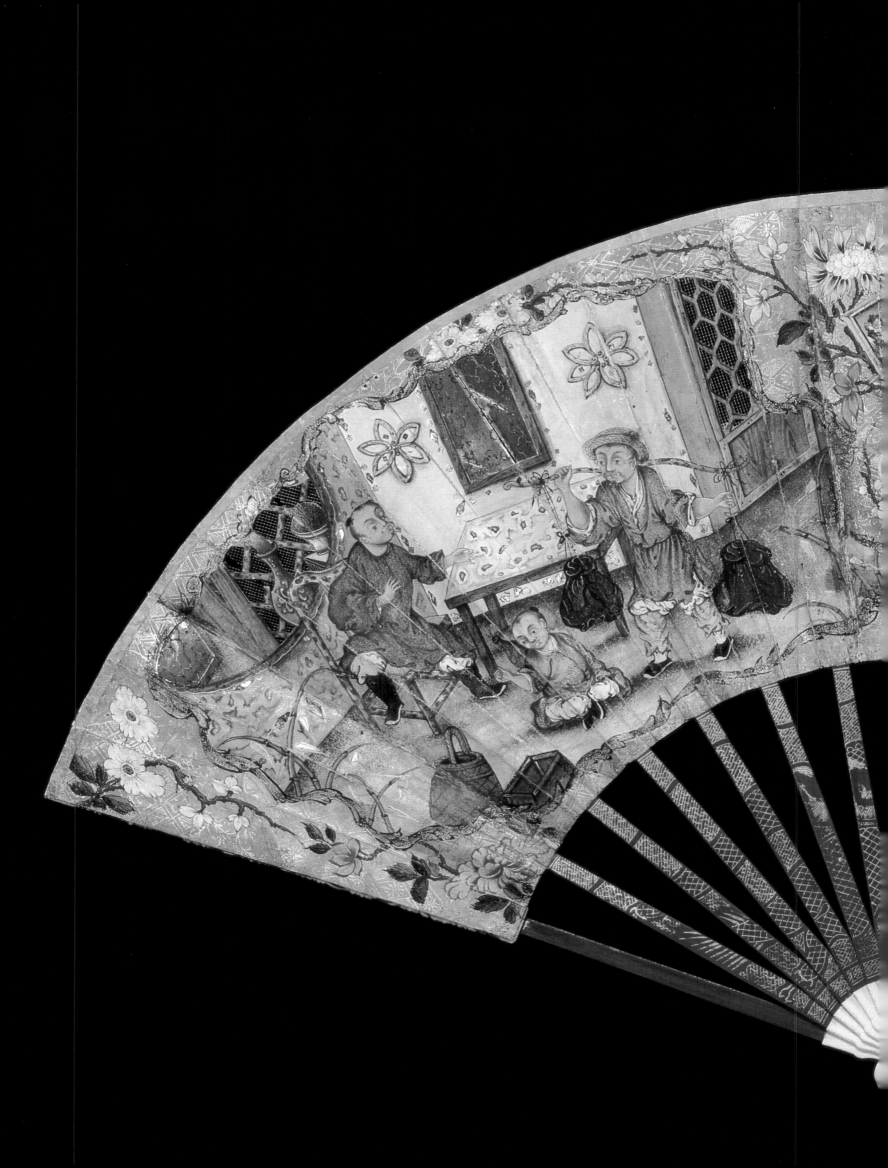

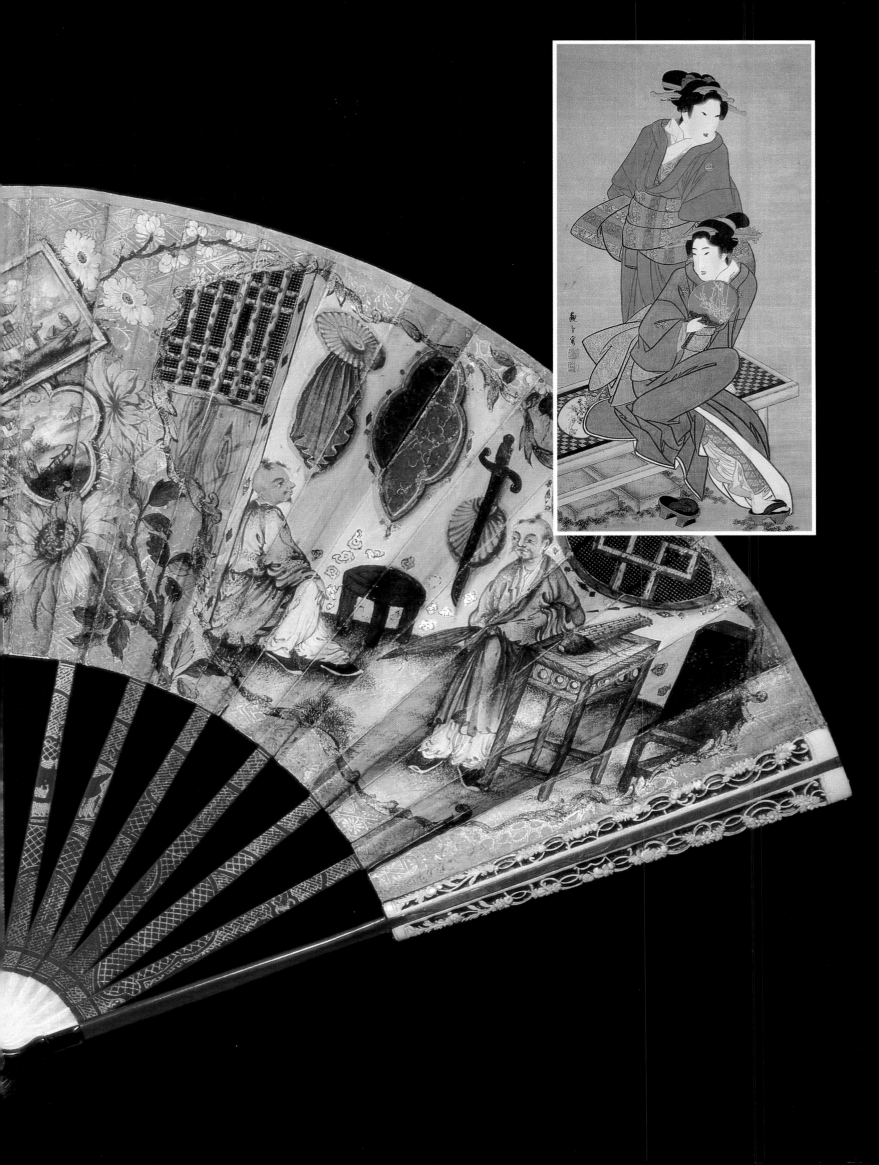

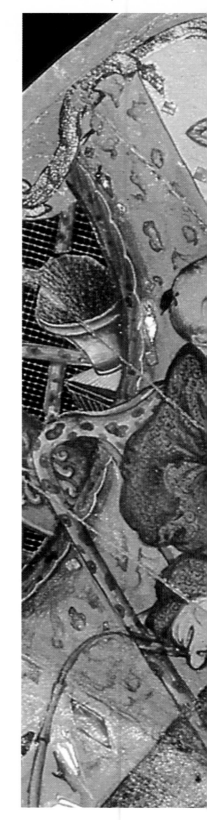

boy next to her playing with a goat (#28) or in other similar examples. An English fan representing a very lively sketch of innocent children's games is also of interest (#53).

Dangerous new events in the area of balloon flight, which people followed with great interest, are also reflected in the motifs of fans. Thus, in the two cartels of a French fan representing a group in a park we see some hot air balloons flying above the picturesque countryside (#17).

The sensational discovery of the cities entombed by Vesuvius (Pompeii and Herculanum) also attracted the attention of painters, in particular the Italians. The master painters in turning more and more often towards antique motifs, towards the theme of the "ruins," they employed ornamental motifs in the spirit of the frescoes of Pompeii. This is clearly observed in the designs of Italian fans from the second half of the 18th century (#'s 58, 59, 61, 62, 63).

Concerning Russian fans, in the 18th century, the mastery of their production did not cede anything to western Europe. The nature of their decoration and their technical execution were done in the spirit of general stylistic tendencies of this period. Moreover, the Russian fans, including those in the collection of Ostankino, are distinguished by their particularities.

In general, in Russian fans, surrounding the disposition of the elements of the decoration there remains still much available space, the background being blank. Usually the small cartels of painting spaced one from the other are united on the sheet in a common composition by delicate ornamental motifs, themselves few in number. And even complete artistic compositions, created in a previous period, are positioned on the sheet with even more space, in a less concentrated fashion and overlaid on the blank background in an organic manner. The difference with French and German fans, for example, the artistic finishing of which distinguishes itself by a great density and great materiality, is that in Russian fans there are richer colors and faded tones. But it is in the details of the blades that the traits and procedures specific to the Russian master engravers are most clearly

109. Back of the fan
painted in the
"chinoiserie" style.
And detail.

seen. The traditional motifs for the engraved embroidery are interpreted and expressed by Russian engravers in a laconic language and imagery, which is to them more familiar and more comprehensible. The details of the engraving follow the painted background of the fan harmoniously and contribute to the unity of the artistic image of the object.

All during the 18th century the fan did not cease to be modified, existing and developing in the framework of determined stylistic tendencies of the period.

During the rococo period, as the feminine costume was considerably modified in form and style, the fan was transformed as well.

In comparison with the baroque period, fashion became lighter, more coquettish, adorned with a multitude of diverse ornaments and imagined with taste. As an integral part of feminine fashion, the fan had to be transformed as well.

Until the middle of the 18th century, it kept its form and decoration specific to the baroque period: large dimensions, narrow and straight blades, a large sheet

112. N. I. Argounov. Portrait of P. I. Cheremetieva in a red shawl, 1801-1802. Museum of Porcelain at the Château Kouskovo. 18th century.

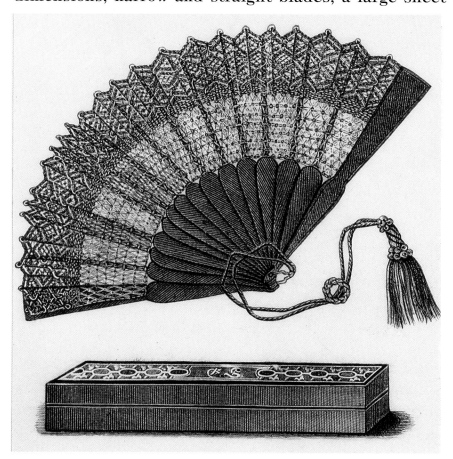

113. Fan with plaited sheet. Fashion engraving from the journal "Modnyi svet" ("The World of Fashion"). 1877.

entirely covered with the composition of a subject similar to a painting. During the rococo period, the fan changed little by little in appearance and conformed to the laws of this style.

Thus, in the 1750's, the character of the design on

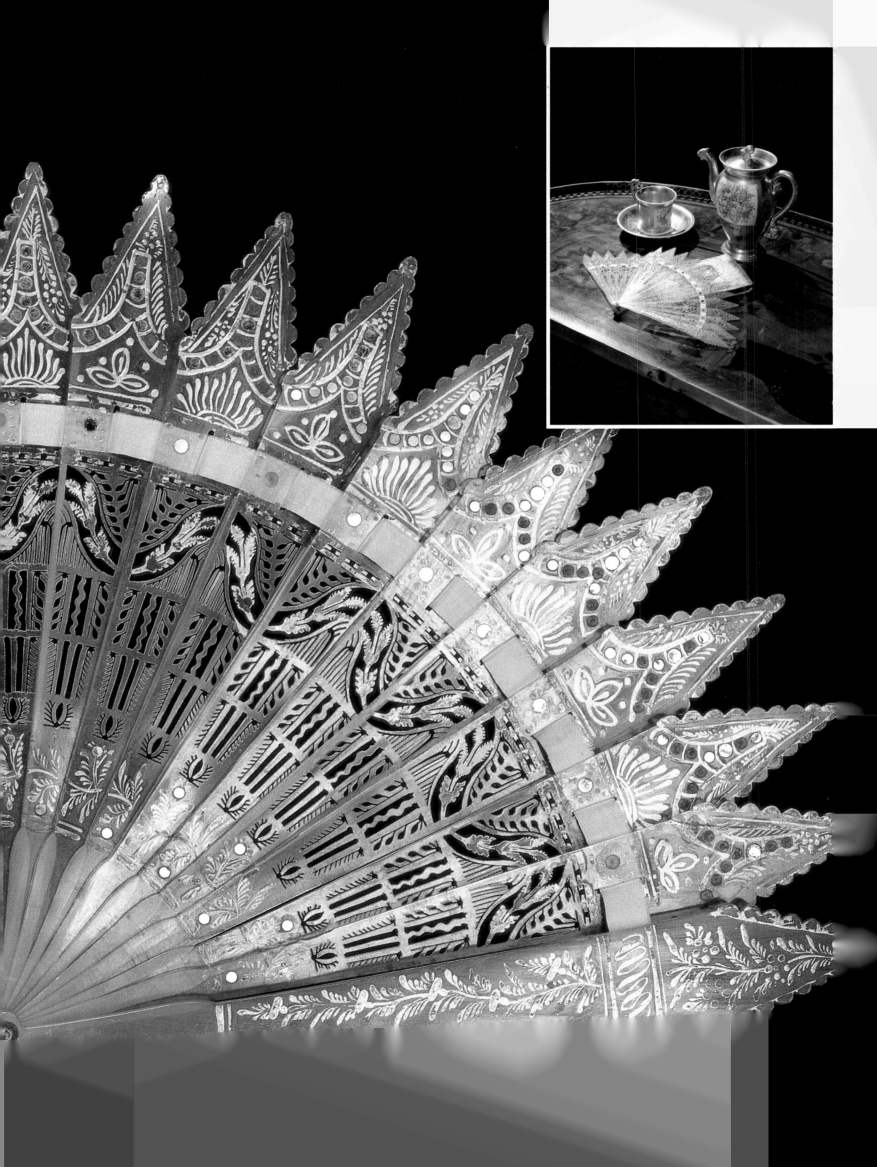

*116. Fashion engraving from the journal, "The Season. Illustrated Ladies Journal."
1870.*

fans itself changed. From being pompous, constricted by its contents and heavy in the manner of its execution, it became lighter and more decorative. In losing its monumental character of yesteryear it became dynamic, ambiguous, and accompanied by a multitude of elegant and original ornamental motifs.

The blades of the frame became lighter as well. They became more open, acquired fantastic contours, distinguished by a rich and varied carving, covered with engravings and enriched with color.

The engraving became fine, so transparent and so skillful that in France, for example, it is considered unlikely that men would be capable of doing such work, which demands extreme attention, great patience and an uncommon attentiveness. This is why in the West, and particularly in France, the engraving was usually left to women. This is believable in taking into account the

117. Fan with five painted cartels Russia (St. Petersburg?). Around 1830.

Preceding pages:

114. Fan with a horn frame, executed in the gothic style and decorated with sequins. Russia. 1820-1830.

115. Fan with a horn frame in the gothic style. Russia. 1820-1830. Teapot and cup from the Batenine factory. 1820's.

information provided by the Encyclopedia of Diderot and Alembert[107].

In Russia too, the account books of Moscow fan factories show that women were called upon to carve bone.

But according to the article by Felkerzam, in France

118. Fashion engraving from the journal, "Der Bazar, illustrierte Damen-Zeitung." 1891.

121. Chinese fan. Middle of the 19th century. Palace of Ostankino in Moscow.

119. Fashion engraving from the journal, "Der Bazar, illustrierte Damen-Zeitung." 1892.

120. Fashion engraving from the journal, "Der Bazar, illustrierte Damen-Zeitung." 1886

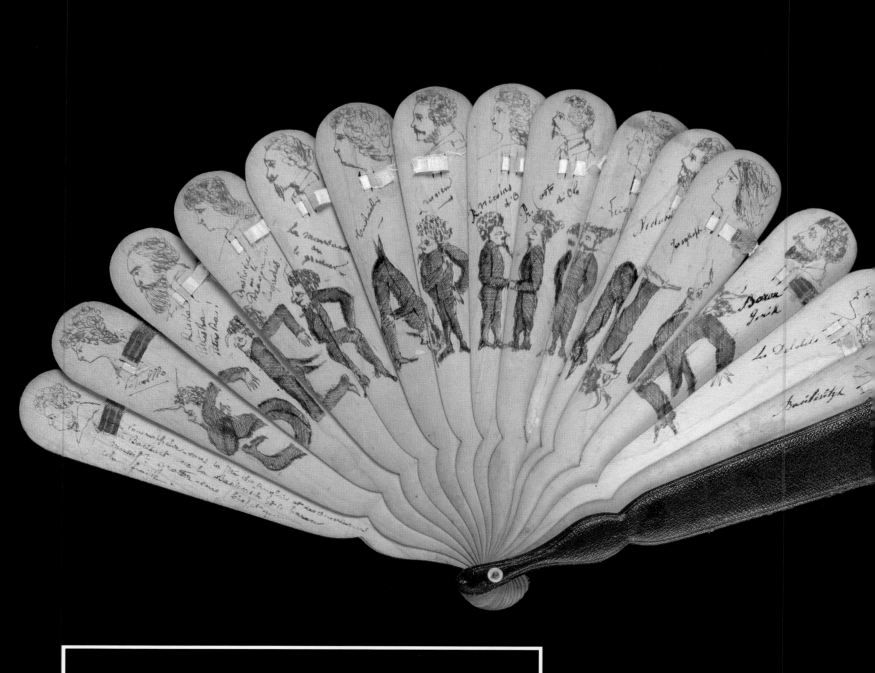

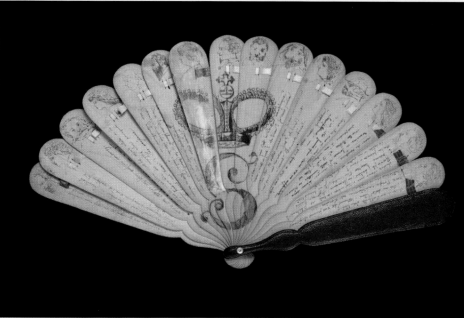

122. *Back of the fan.*

123. *Fan with a wood frame painted in ink. Russia. 1850-1860.*

during the 1780's, a certain Mademoiselle Pinter[108] excelled more than other women in the creation of openwork carving. During this period fans were so appreciated that they began to be offered as gifts to the nobility. They became one of the elements in the outfits of fiancées of high society and were among the number of gifts that the future husbands gave their beloved. It was certainly the custom of the French court. But this was also the practice in Russia. Thus, after the victory of Tchesmenska, Grigori Orlov gave Catherine II a fan, the gold blades of which had been produced by the master Ador and the sheet painted in the theme of famous battles by the professor of history and painter G. I. Kozlov[109]. In the trunk which contained the dowry of Marie Lechtchinskaïa, the future Queen of France, were found 35 fans made by Tikke, the master of the court, valued at 3,627 pounds[110]. In 1745, at the time of the marriage of the dauphin and the infant Marie-

124. Fashion engraving from the journal, "Townsbend's Monthly Selection of Parisian Costumes." 1833

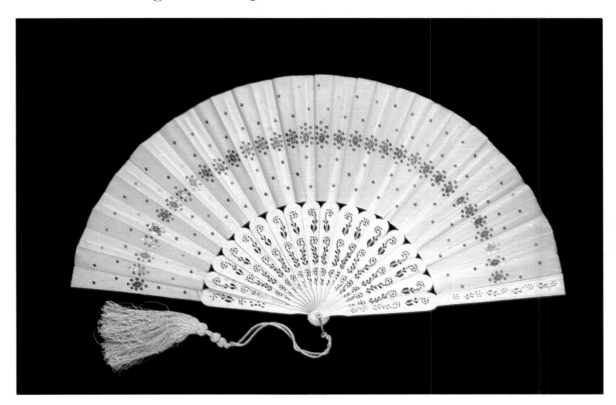

Therese-Antoinette of Spain, the latter received, among other gifts, 36 fans at a value of 3,855 pounds[111].

In the second half of the 18th century, we observe a new development in classicism which was also reflected in the art of fans. Of a narrative character, its design became more decorative, the blades of the frame were no longer close together. In the 1760's, the sheet became thinner and the blades seemed to get longer. In the 1770's, the feminine costume lightened even more, became shorter, pressing up against the body in the manner of a lampshade, decorated with refinements of

125. Fan with a silk sheet decorated with sequins. Russia. Around 1870.

95

126. Fashion engraving from the journal, "Parisian Fashions. Office of Historic Fashions and Costumes." 1828.

ribbons, knots, and of diverse garlands. At the same time the form of the fan was radically transformed. Its dimensions diminished considerably in comparison with those of the 1750's. The blades became shorter, the sheet narrower. The design, which at one time took up the entire sheet, now disappeared and, as with its composition, became clean and symmetrical, divided into distinct cartels. Ornamental embroidery filled up the empty space. In order to further fill the space of the sheet, scintillating sequins of all colors were introduced in abundance as well as silk threads.

The blades became straight and narrow, and further apart, permitting an original game of light and shadow. It is not by accident if, in France, the characteristic fan frames of the period were labeled with humor as "skeletons"[112].

Two Russian models of the 1770's, "The Rendezvous in the Park" and "The Knight with the Lady in the Park" (#'s 3 and 4) are examples of fans of this type. The rather narrow sheets of these two examples are fixed to lengthened narrow blades, each one a little further

127. Fan with a silk sheet painted with little flowers. Russia. Around 1870.

Following pages:

128. Fan in painted lace. Russia. Around 1870. And detail.

removed from the next. They are covered with engravings and inlaid with silver. Compared with fans of western Europe, the engraving which decorates the frame is parsimonious, severe but executed with great craftsmanship and skill with a sense of the medium and the great knowledge of the materials used. Even the more abundant decoration of the second fan is not contrary to the harmony and the general stylistic principles of the whole. The art of the bone sculptors fits marvelously with the classical style of the design

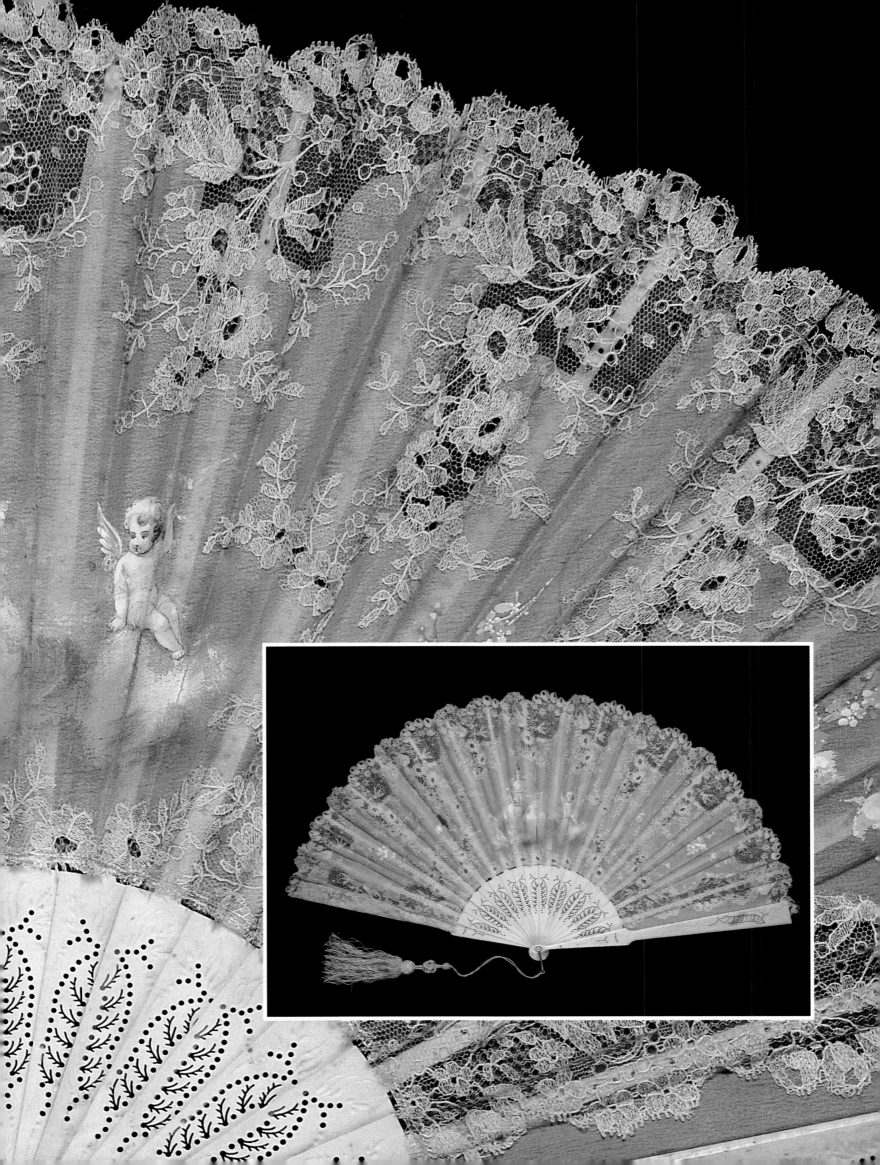

of the sheet, the cartels of which represent subjects positioned in a clean and symmetrical fashion. One can regard them as medallions painted independently suspended on the face of the sheet and framed by garlands of flowers. The composition of the whole is constructed with the aid of parsimonious methods, but very expressive, with a cleanly dominating decorative base.

Compared to Russian fans, the decoration of fans of western Europe from this period, even if they were produced according to the same rules, were executed in a denser manner, more abundant, with a sometimes inordinate use of diverse decorative elements simultaneously.

This process can certainly be seen in the second half of the 18th century when, in the decoration of fans along with other elements, embroidery with threads of

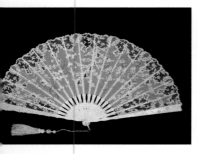

129. Fan in silk and lace, decorated with a painting representing bees and flowers. Russia. Around 1880.

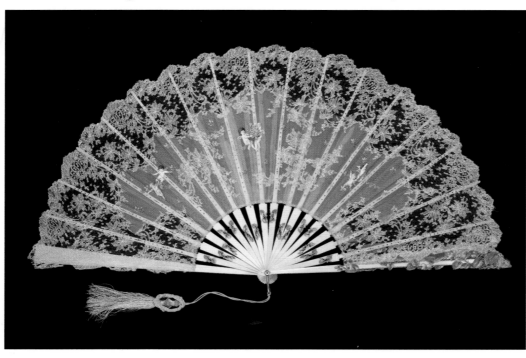

130. Fan in lace representing frolicking lovers. Russia. 1880's.

silk or even metal was introduced more and more often. In the ornamental and pictorial compositions of the sheets, metallic sequins in tones of gold or silver were inserted in the most diverse shapes. This can be noted, for example, on the French fans "The Bird-Sellers in Love" (#13), "The Pastoral" (#14) and "The Rendezvous" (#19).

Near the end of the 18th century, sequins were so abundantly employed on fans, in England for example, that they constitute alone nearly the entire subject of the ornamental composition. These were produced in a rather impressive manner and with a great understanding of the specificity of this material; such as the English

131. Fan in white ostrich feathers.
Russia. Around 1880.

Following pages:

132. Satin fan representing a bouquet.
Russia. Around 1880.

133. Fan sheet, made in silk gauze and lace,
carrying a design of bouquets of edelweiss and
branches of flowers.
Russia. Around 1880.

134. Satin fan, with a design of flowers, carrying
the inscription "Souvenir."
Russia. 1880-1890.

135. Fan, with a blue silk sheet, decorated with an
embroidery and lace appliquée.
Russia. Around 1890.

136. Fan with a frame of openwork bone.
Russia. End of the 19th century.

137. Nicolas II and Alexandra Fédorovna. 1895.

fans of the collection of the Palace of Ostankino, entirely decorated in sequins and in silk thread (#'s 54-56), to which blades polished like mirrors are attached and with paste on the panaches imitating precious stones (#54).

In the 1790's, the dimensions of fans diminished considerably, so much so that they earned the name "Lilliputians"[113]. Their blades once again came close together and the correspondence between the proportions of the frame

and the sheet, despite their new dimensions, recalled that which existed in the large fans of the first half of the century. Fans conserved this appearance until the beginning of the 19th century.

In the 18th century, we observe in the art of fan decoration the following particularity: despite the fact that the form and the decoration of the fan had evolved conforming to the fluctuations of the tendencies in style and decor, the process of their decoration had visibly conserved a certain independence and originality by getting a little ahead of the development of the feminine costume.

Thus, even during the period of the spread of the baroque and rococo styles, traits of classicism in the decoration of fans are clearly seen. This is clearly seen, for example, in the Russian fan of three cartels (#1) dating from the middle of the 18th century. Its carving and the nature of its design reveal dominating traits of the rococo style. But the clean, symmetric disposition of the cartels and their decorative frames reflect an influence of classicism. This orientation in the decoration of fans developed with a clarity which was specific to the 1770's.

One can explain this particularity by the fact that the fan, although being by its nature one of the accessories of women's fashion, compared to other components of the ornamentation of dress, represented the most mobile part, the most active and the most expressive of the costume, which gave it in some way the right to a more independent existence.

This particularity can also be explained by the expression of the laws referred to by researchers: the coexistence of different stylistic tendencies which appear at the end of the 17th century continue through to the beginning of the 18th century[114].

In the second half of the 18th century, as we have already said, in Russia the fan became an accessory so necessary during ceremonies, balls and receptions that it in some ways lost its initial utilitarian function and it became an instrument of the most refined coquetries. The art of handling a fan demanded a lot of know-how, ingenuity and dexterity. It is not by accident that the famous writer Madame de Staël professed that she could easily distinguish a princess from a countess, and a marquise from a commoner by the manner in which she would use her fan and that, of all the objects making

140. Fan in black ostrich feathers.
Russia. End of the 19th century.

141. Lace fan.
Russia. End of the 19th century.

Preceding pages:

138. Karl Brullov.
Portrait of the princess Elizaveta
Saltykova, 1841.
Oil on canvas, 200 x 142 cm.
Russian Museum, St. Petersburg.

139. Fan, with embroidery of flowers,
stitched with sequins on a silk sheet.
Russia (France?). Around 1890.

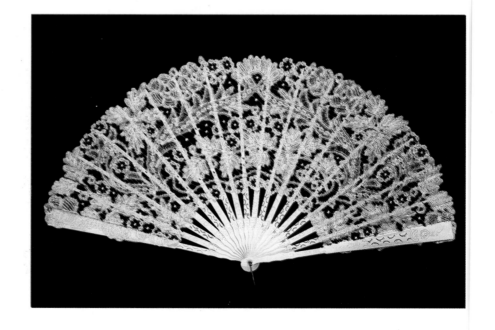

up the wardrobe of a woman of fashion, none could be used as smartly as a fan[115].

During this period a whole assortment of fan manipulations was developed, indispensable to test and attract admirers and worshipers. In skillful hands, a fan would become a reliable means to emphasize the charms of a beautiful woman or to hide her faults. It is not an accident that the owners of fans themselves would call it their "useful zephyr" or "the screen of prudence"[116].

In 1790, one could read in the "Satiritcheskyi vestnik" ("The Satirical Journal"), published by the famous editor of the period P. I. Strakhov: "One recognizes the great talents of beautiful women in the number of times in which they shake their fans so that the little scarf covering the breast adopts the charming position

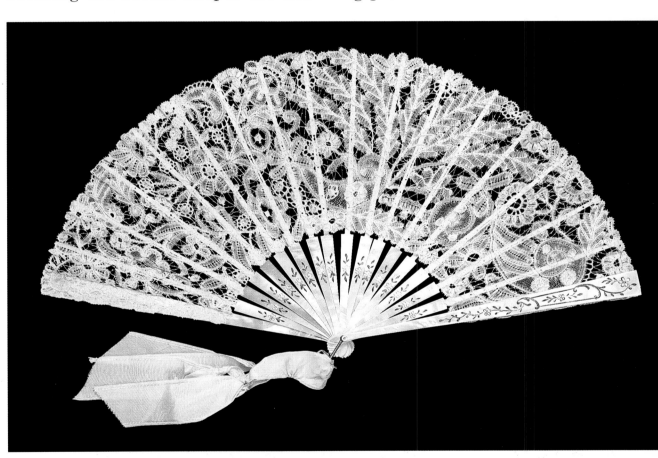

which permits, despite the pins, it to seem like an inconvenience; they know also how many shakes of the fan are necessary to close this scarf or how many are necessary to agreeably tussle their hair in order that it takes on that ravishing position that only a fan, and no mortal hand, can obtain for them"[117].

To put her admirers to the test, a belle would drop her fan and attentively observe their reactions. Certainly the chivalry of the first gentleman to pick up the fan would be held close to her heart and the "winner" would

142. Lace fan.
Russia.
End of the 19th century.

107

143. Fashion engraving
carrying the
inscription, "Walking
dress. R. Ackepman's
repository of arts."
1821

144. Fan with a sheet
of silk and lace.
Russia. End of the
19th century.

receive awaited reward. The fan often played the role of a carrier of love messages. A fan forgotten "by accident" would hold sweet notes which were transmitted to the object of her adoration[118].

The fan often served as a sort of "library" of love poems, aphorisms, songs or of scores. The works drawn or fixed on the back of the fan amused people attending a party or a reception, helping their owners to shine or to show them as spiritual[119]. It is not by accident if, in France in the 18th century, that the aphorism appeared, "the fan of a belle is the scepter of the world"[120]

The fan was so popular that it bred in fashionable society ambiguous aphorisms, epigrams and puns. Thus, a pun, generally spoken by gentlemen, was in style in France:

"I took your fan, Madame, but do not be in ire;
Think upon my ardor, consider my fire,
You will see that I have more need of it than you"[121].

In albums one would write acrostics in which the first letter of each line formed the word "éventail" (French for fan). Here is an example:

145. Fan made of pheasant
feathers.
Russia. End of the 19th
century.

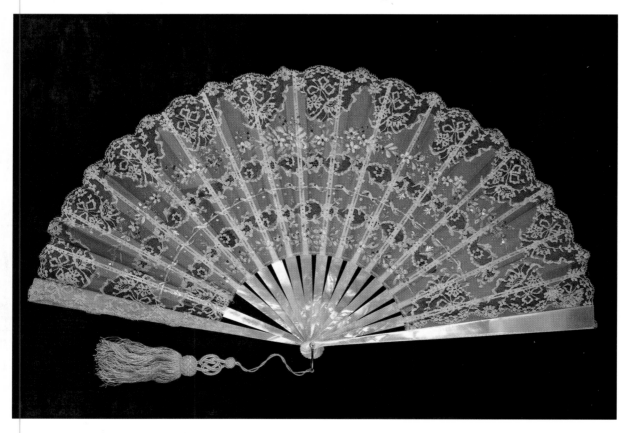

Eve n'a point connu mon élégant travail;
Eve hardly knew my elegant work;
Vénus m'imagina, Le féminin bercail,
Venus imagined me, The female fold,
Et maint peuple rôti qui tout cru mange l'ail,

Following pages:

146. Fan with a sheet of black
watered fabric.
Russia. End of the 19th
century.

Following double pages:

147. Lace fan, monogrammed
A. A. Tatischeva.
Russia. End of the 19th
century.

148. Fan representing a
bouquet of flowers.
Russia. End of the 19th
century – beginning of the
20th century.

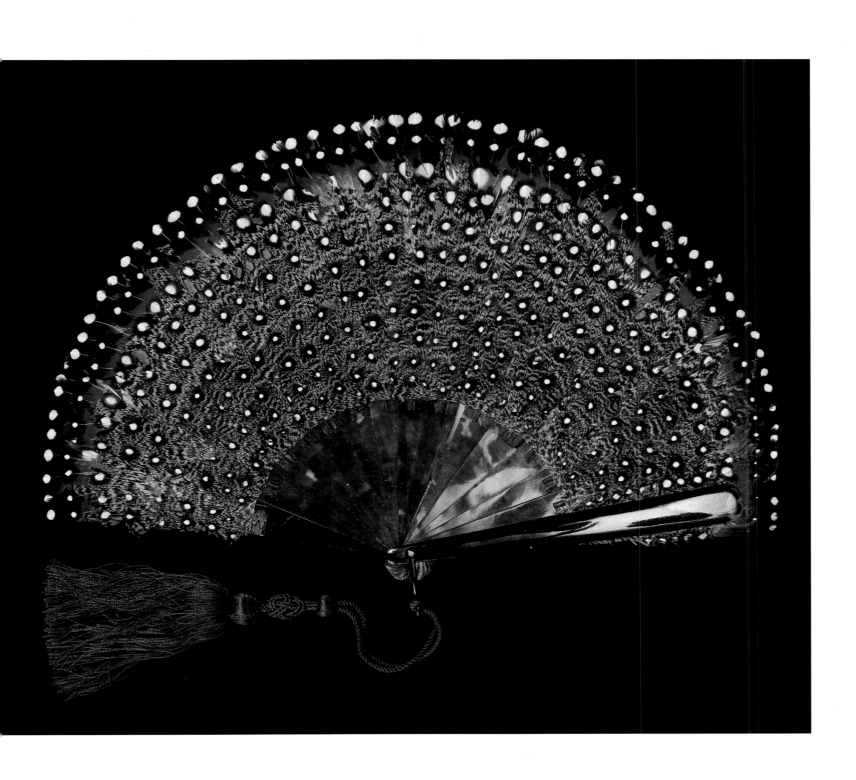

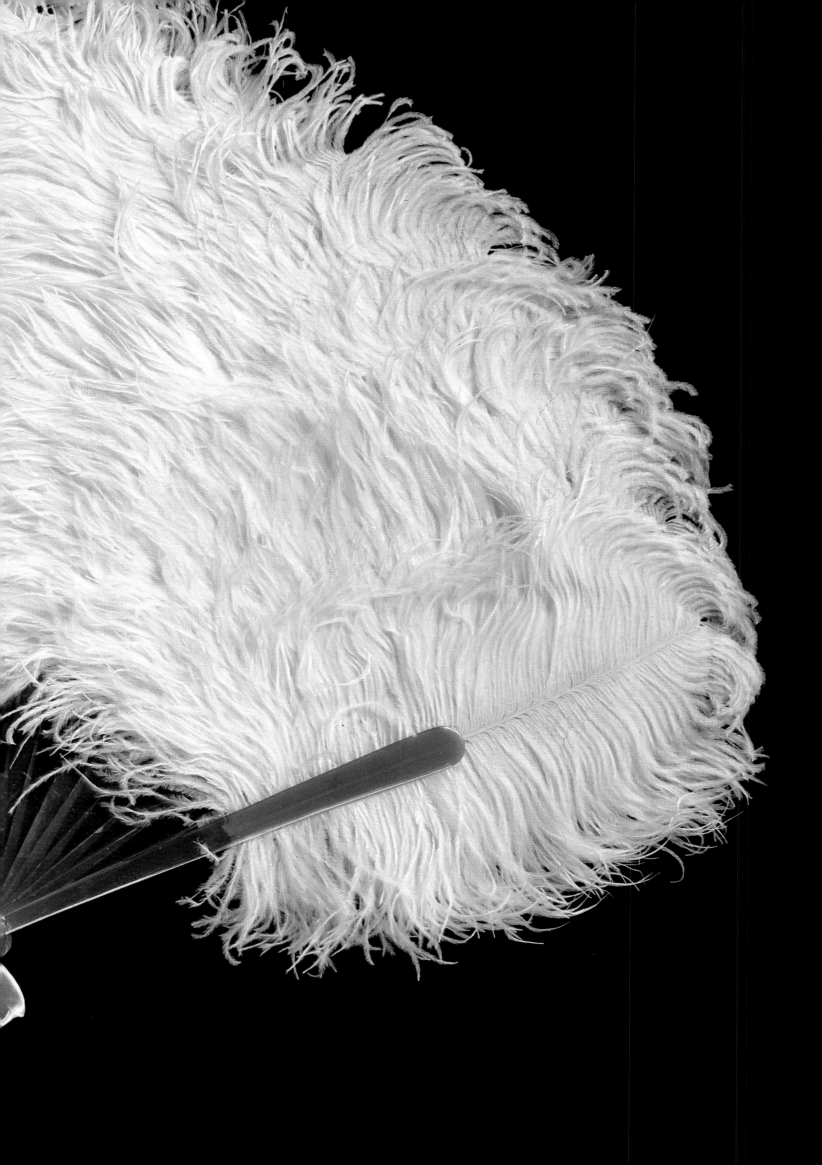

151. Two-sided wedding
fan. Frame of 20 blades
in openwork mother-of-
pearl. Painted by
Calamatta from motifs
of the painter Picou.
France. About 1870.
28 x 60 cm.
Arrived in 1981, from
the Museum of
Porcelain, in the
Château Kouskovo, from
the 18th century.
Coming from the
collection of L. I.
Rouszkaïa.

*And many roasting people who all have an eye
for fashion,*
Nérine à l'Opéra, Fatmé dans le Sérail,
Nerine at the Opera, Fatmé in the seraglio,
Trouvent dans mon secours un utile attirail
Find in my aid a useful tool
A l'aide de mon jeu, savant dans son détail.
With the help of my game, knowing in its detail.
Iris a plus d'un coeur a fait faire un long bail.
*Iris has more than a heart which is made to remain
faithful too long.*
Le sceptre d'une belle est vraiment L'Eventail"[122].
The scepter of a belle is truly the Fan.

In the works of Russian writers and poets the fan
played the role of a symbol, a metaphor and an actor.
One can cite, for example, a poem by G. R. Derjavine
written in 1780 entitled "The Fan."
"If I possessed the entire Earth

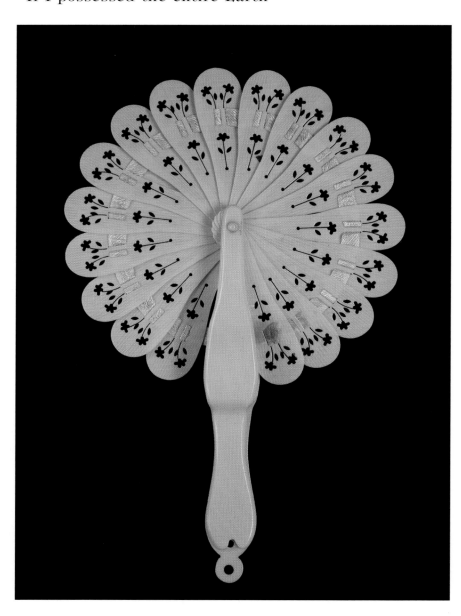

Preceding pages:

149. Fan with a sheet of
blue feathers.
Russia. End of the 19th
century – beginning of
the 20th century.

150. Fan, with a sheet
of white ostrich feathers.
Russia. End of the 19th
century – beginning of
the 20th century.

152. Fan, in the form of a screen,
frame in gutta-percha, carrying an
engraving of flowers.
Russia. End of the 19th century –
beginning of the 20th century.

I would be a fan. My breeze would refresh the whole
world
And I would be a shield for the universe;
And you Chloé, upon fluttering me,
Sighing from the strong heat,

You would be radiant like a sun
And beautiful thanks to my shadow."
   In 1805, appearing in the press was the fable of the
famous Russian poet I. I. Dmitriev, "Two Fans" of
which the characters were talking fans:
"Two fans were sitting on the table of a salon;
I don't know to whom they belonged,
But I do know that one was new, beautiful, covered
with sequins;
The second all broken and boasting a lot about it.
'To whom do you belong,' he asked proudly of his
neighbor.
'To a woman,' the other responded courteously.
'Well I serve a beautiful woman,' said the braggart,
And how I serve her! See, not a blade intact!
As soon as a young man approaches for audacious talk

*153. Two-sided fan:
"Rural Wedding."
Ukraine. 1860's.*

117

154. Pierre Bonnard
*Poster France-Champagne,
1891.
Lithograph in color.*

Bang! I hit him! In a word,
Believe me, without meaning to brag,
And this is not a reproach,
But each of my movements
Witness the consistency of Vetrana.'
Her coquetries and her silly fluttering, do not they
deserve better?
Said his neighbor, 'It suffices for my Rosalie
A look, and all respect her."[123].

This refinement in the use of the fan gave birth to a special language called "the art of fluttering one's fan." This was a method of expressing one's sentiments, humors, opinions and intentions. Moreover, there existed a very great quantity of manipulations. Evidently, it required the development of much effort to assimilate but a few of them[124].

The following play on words, which became popular, was composed in the spirit of this language: "It is not fashionable to love only one man. In our days one waves about in the function of time"[125].

The language of the fan became so widespread that in Russia the word "agitation" acquired at the end of the 18th century the sense of "bureaucracy"[126].

Thus, for example, V. N. Zinoviev, who went to Rome

156. Edouard Manet.
*Music in the Tuileries, 1862.
Whole and detail view.
National Gallery, London.*

157. Léon Bonnat.
*Madame Léopold Stern,
1879.
Musée Bonnat, Bayone.*

155. Fan:
*"Family Scene."
France. Beginning of the
19th century.*

in 1785, recounts in these terms the stay in that city of the prince N. B. Ioussoupov: "I found here our two ministers Ioussoupov and Razoumovski. The first had not changed: he bought very ugly paintings (. . .) fluttered about as much here as in Turin, in a word, he remained the same"[127].

During the same period, tired of the traditional methods of predicting the future such as cards or coffee grounds, the fashionable women invented a new one with the help of fans. As described in the "Satirical

118

Journal," the women assembled together closed fans, loaned by the women in the group, and, in taking one at random, they would make predictions based on the representation on the sheet or the number of blades of the frame[128].

The facts just enumerated show well the role and the significance of the fan in the life of fashionable society of the period.

In the 18th century, along with the folding fan, the most widespread type, there existed other variants of this accessory. We know that in the apartments of the palaces of Russia and Western Europe, as well as in houses, there were, for example, fireplace fans. These served to procure coolness and to protect from the heat people conversing next to the fire.

In the inventory of the Marble Palace of St. Petersburg, compiled in 1705, is listed for nearly each fireplace: "a fan in paper printed with a painting, fitted with a handle in wood, half gilded and half covered with taffeta"[129].

The sheets of this type of screen were made of diverse materials: fabric, wood, paper-maché, etc. In The Hermitage Museum, for example, two Russian fans are conserved from the second half of the 18th century, the sheets of which are wood, painted with multicolored laquer in the "chinoiserie" style[130].

Symphony in White. No III. Whistler 67.

But the fireplace screens were most often made of sheets of cardboard decorated with painting or engraving and mounted on a handle of chiseled wood. The collection of Ostankino also displays fans of this type. There are two Russian fans forming a pair dating from the end of the 18th century – beginning of the 19th century, coming to the museum in 1936 from The Hermitage (#'s 6 and 7). The beautiful oval sheets of these fireplace screens are adorned with golden scrolls and with sheets which come together at branches of green oaks, framing the

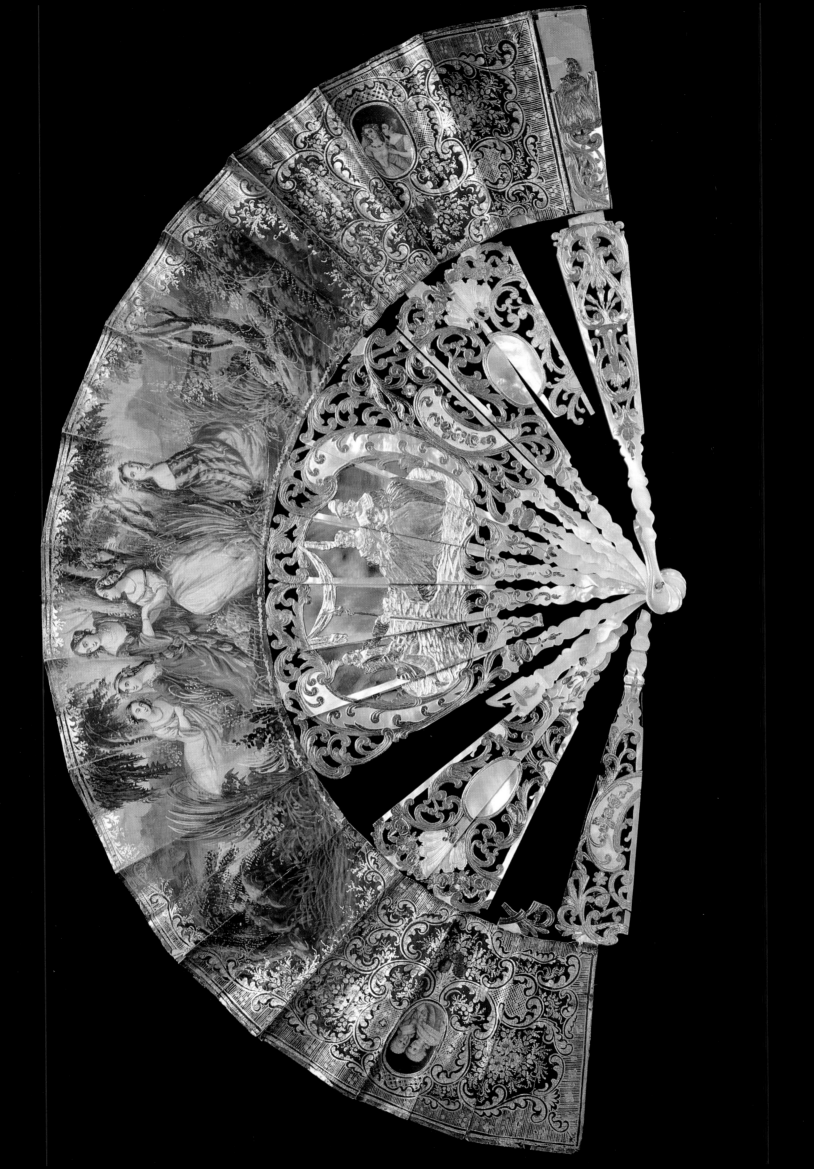

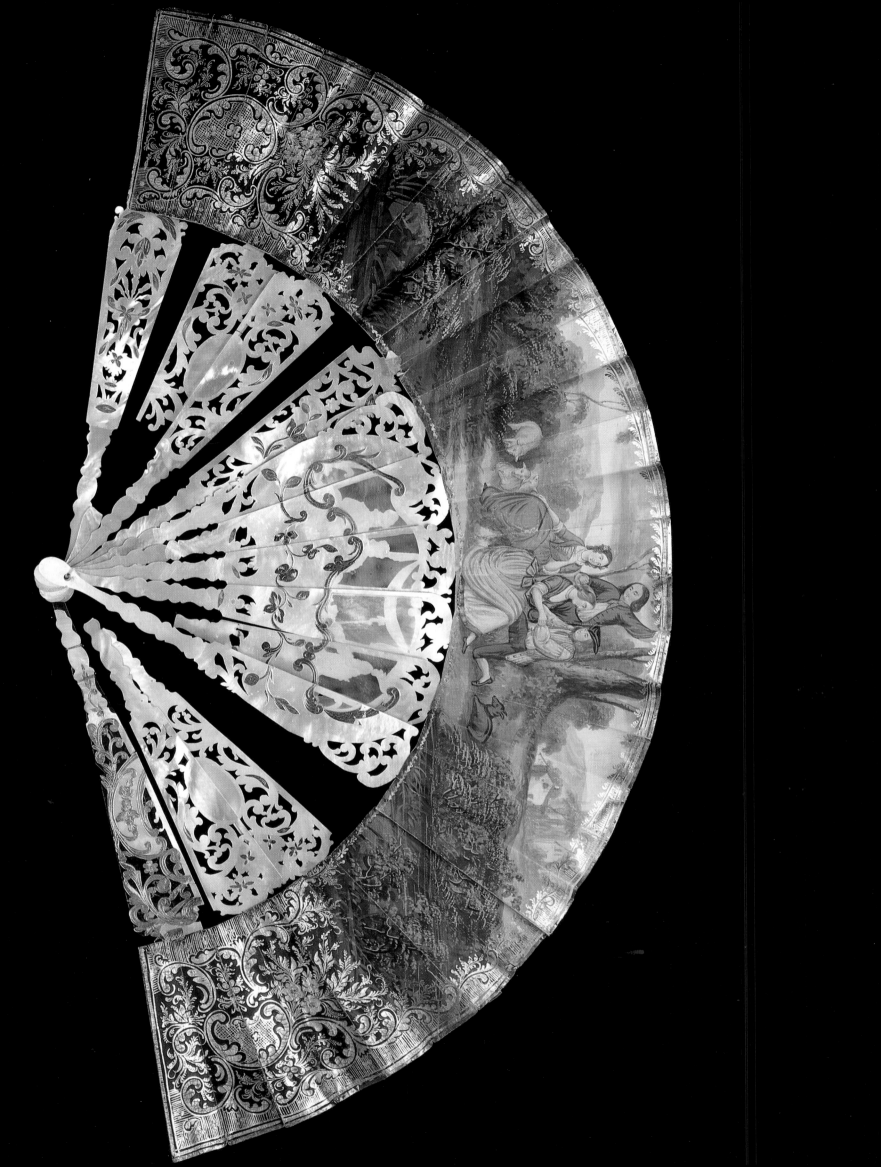

motif of a drawing without pretension, forming a harmonious composition in the overall decor of the fan. Handles in a carved and gilded wood, of lovely form, complete the decoration of these fans.

It is necessary to note that aside from the types of screens mentioned above, there existed still another type, which were called theater screens due to their sheets, decorated with motif compositions, with texts and scores placed on the back. In effect, certain screens of this type in the collection of the Palace of Ostankino are equipped with sheets decorated with engravings, which represent scenes from various plays on one side and extracts of dialogue on the other (#'s 22-26).

The theater screens were especially made in France and then exported to other countries, where sometimes were added such details as the handles and the drawing, surrounding the engraving or texts. These were produced, in particular, in Russia. According to all sources, it is in Russia that these objects were called theater screens because in other countries, and particularly in France, they always remained fireplace screens and carry

Preceding pages:

164. Two-sided fan: "The Young Sirens." France. Middle of the 19th century.

165. Back of the fan.

166. Fan: "Gallant Scene." France. Middle of the 19th century.

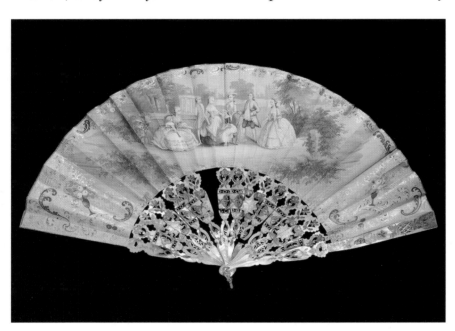

167. Two-sided fan, representing a scene of rural life. France. Middle of the 19th century. And detail.

this name still today. We find, for example, the reproduction of a fireplace screen, the form and decoration of which resemble that of some theater screens from the collection of Ostankino, based on the engraving by A. Romaneïa, produced from the drawing by J. M. Moreau, "The Little Washstand." This drawing represents a well placed person having her morning wash and holding in her hand a screen of the style of the theater screens[131].

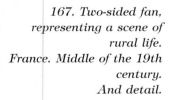

126

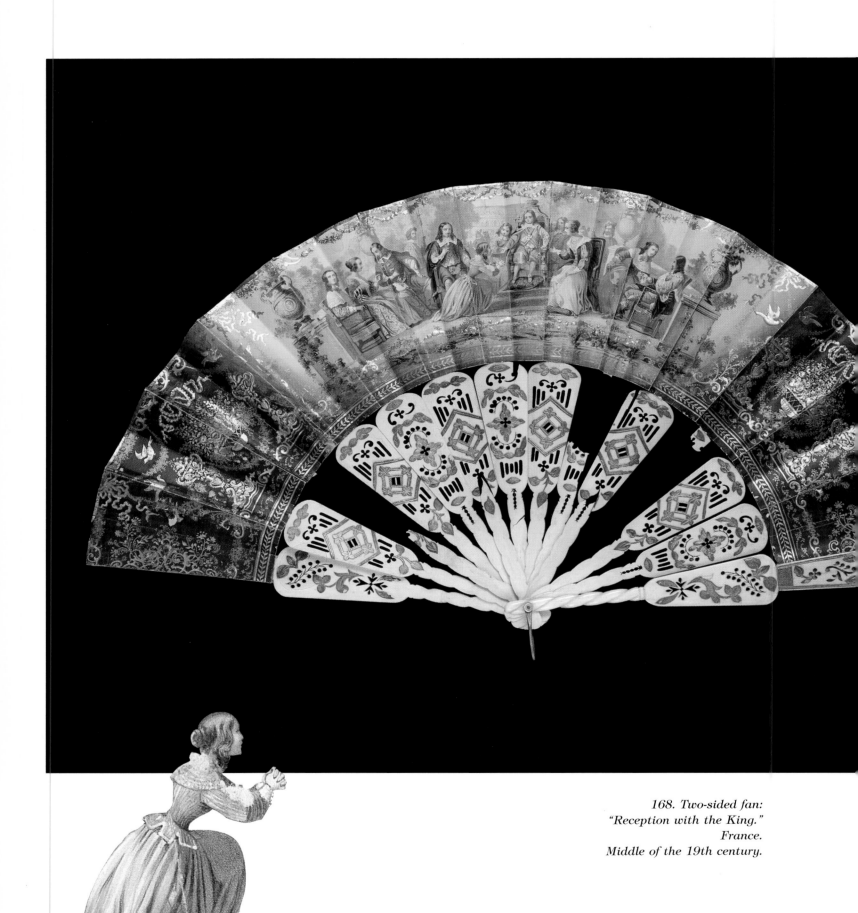

*168. Two-sided fan:
"Reception with the King."
France.
Middle of the 19th century.*

Theatre screens were used with pleasure in Russia, in particular by the owners of private theatres. They could be found in the lobbies of theatres, all the more so since the theme of their decoration coincided with the function of the buildings in which they were used.

There were also fireplace fans in the theater rooms of the Palace of Ostankino. This is known because according to the palace inventory, dating from 1802, in which is written that next to the fireplaces, among other accessories, were found fans[132]. Thus, in the passage gallery leading to the Italian pavilion, next to the fireplace, "four paper fans fitted with wood handles"[133] And in the Italian pavilion itself, next to four fireplaces, were found "forty-four paper fans carrying insignias, presenting on one side some phrases in French and on the other some characters"[134]. The family of V. P. Cheremetiev, the direct descendant of the founder of the Palace of Ostankino, the Count Cheremetiev, conserved four examples of fireplace fans from the theatre up to 1979 (#'s 22, 23, 25, 26). Today, the museum's collection of fans contains seven of this type.

At the beginning of the 19th century, the Empire style established itself. And the fan, being an integral part of the feminine costume, followed the dominant fashion. During this period, dresses were created from thinner

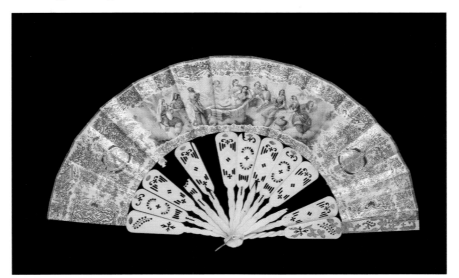

169. Back of the fan.

fabrics (batiste, crÍpe, muslin, silk) in pastel tones. The cuts were lengthened, holding the waist tightly, as to imitate antique models. The silhouettes and the volumes were clearly distinguished from the previous century. It is true that these tendencies were already noticeable towards the end of the 18th century during the period of "Directory" style, which was largely reflected in the form and decoration of the fan. At the

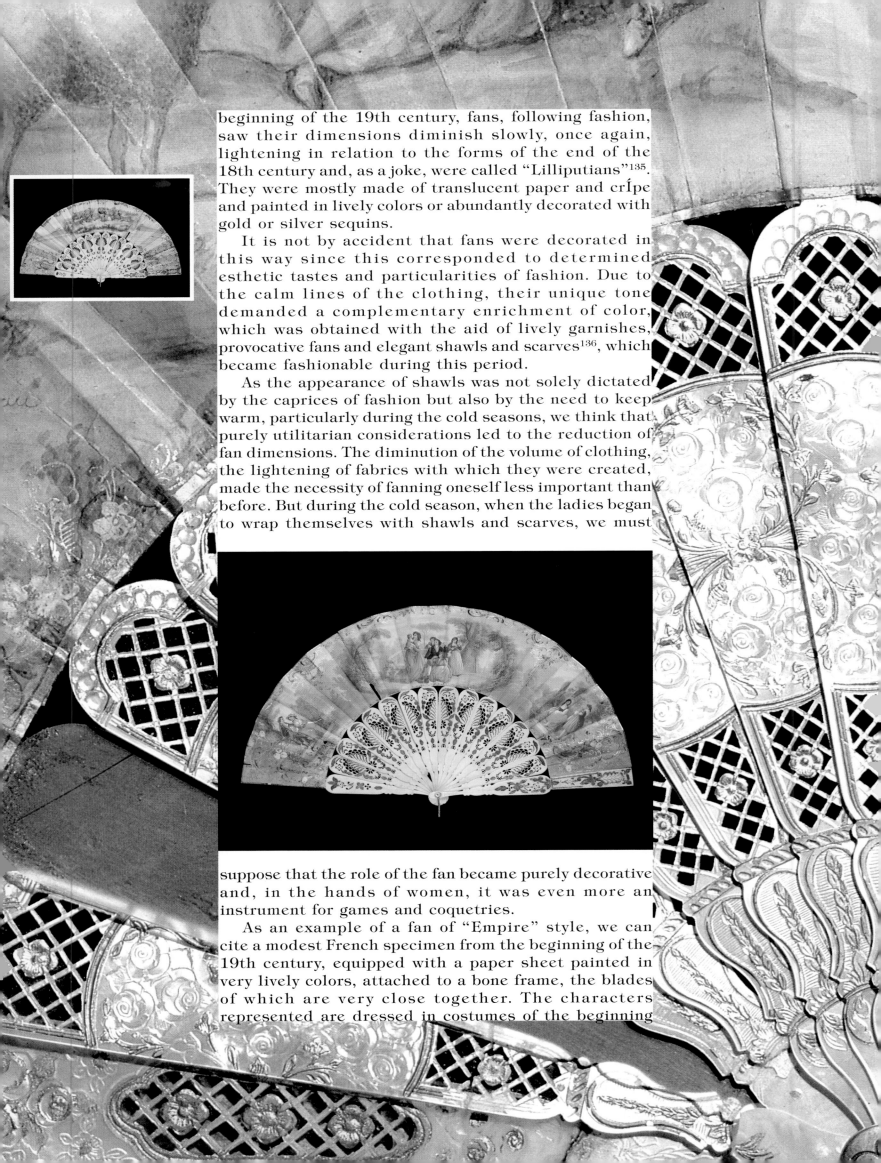

beginning of the 19th century, fans, following fashion, saw their dimensions diminish slowly, once again, lightening in relation to the forms of the end of the 18th century and, as a joke, were called "Lilliputians"[135]. They were mostly made of translucent paper and crípe and painted in lively colors or abundantly decorated with gold or silver sequins.

It is not by accident that fans were decorated in this way since this corresponded to determined esthetic tastes and particularities of fashion. Due to the calm lines of the clothing, their unique tone demanded a complementary enrichment of color, which was obtained with the aid of lively garnishes, provocative fans and elegant shawls and scarves[136], which became fashionable during this period.

As the appearance of shawls was not solely dictated by the caprices of fashion but also by the need to keep warm, particularly during the cold seasons, we think that purely utilitarian considerations led to the reduction of fan dimensions. The diminution of the volume of clothing, the lightening of fabrics with which they were created, made the necessity of fanning oneself less important than before. But during the cold season, when the ladies began to wrap themselves with shawls and scarves, we must

suppose that the role of the fan became purely decorative and, in the hands of women, it was even more an instrument for games and coquetries.

As an example of a fan of "Empire" style, we can cite a modest French specimen from the beginning of the 19th century, equipped with a paper sheet painted in very lively colors, attached to a bone frame, the blades of which are very close together. The characters represented are dressed in costumes of the beginning

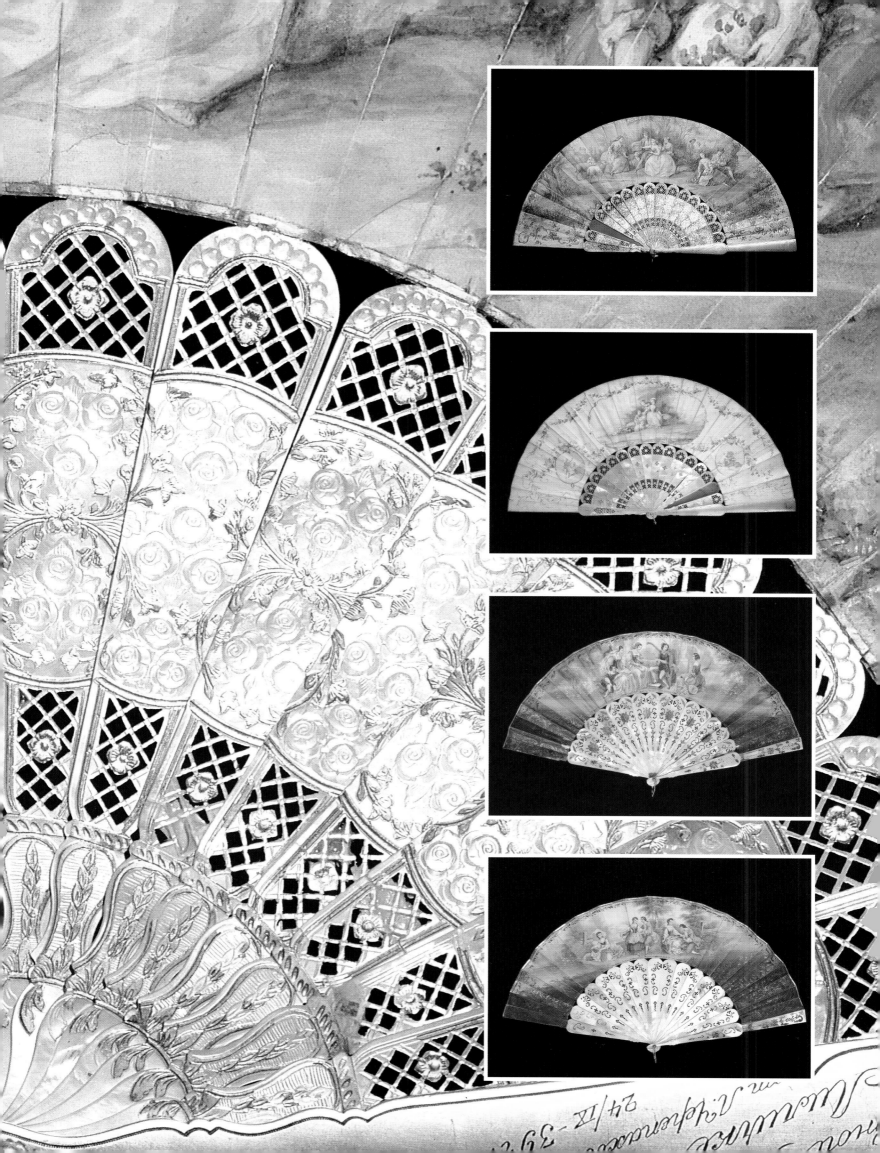

of the 19th century, executed in the "Empire" style (#95). At the beginning of the century, although the skill with which the fan was used in the second half of the 18th century was lost, this accessory continued to play an independent role, and skill in its use acquired a great importance. Special schools were created to teach this art, like dancing schools. For example, in London, just at the beginning of the century, an upper class lady founded "The Academy of the Art of Using a Fan"[137].

During the course of its following development, the fan did not cease to be subjected to transformations, conforming to the evolution of tastes, of novelties, introduced by fashion into dress and the objects of daily life. After 1806, in the 1810's, thicker fabrics began to be used for women's fashions. These were abundantly decorated with embroidery and appliqués. Around 1820,

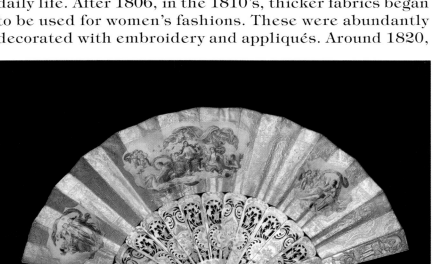

the most popular tones began to be attributed with fantastic names in the fashion of sentimental humor of the period: "the unconscious frog", "the toad in love", "the dreaming flea", or "the spider contemplating his victim"[138].

The fans of this period were also made in paper and cloth of a tone more dense. They were decorated with designs created under the influences in vogue in art and literature: sentimentalism and romanticism. In the 1820's, we find allegories representing temples of friendship, weeping willows framed with flowers and little palm leaves being the dominating theme; they are often stitched with colored silk and

Page to the right

180. Fan:
"The Rendezvous."
France. 1870-1880.
And detail.

sequins. Some folding fans entirely fabricated in bone, horn or shell appear. They also reflect the infatuation for the gothic style, in vogue during this period. For example, we can cite the fans of the collection of the Museum of Ostankino. One of these, produced in Russia, is made entirely of blades in horn. It was created under the influence of gothic motifs, which were very widespread in Russian art during this period. The soft brown color of the 22 dentaled blades in the gothic style is harmoniously decorated with rare sequins and golden paint. The whole gives an impression of severe archaism.

A fan from Western Europe, created in the gothic style in the 1820's and made of blades of bone, abundantly decorated with a polychrome design, leaves a lively

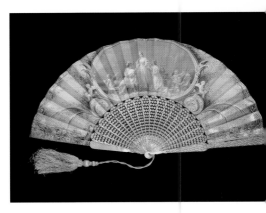

178. Wedding fan, painted on both sides. France. Around 1870.

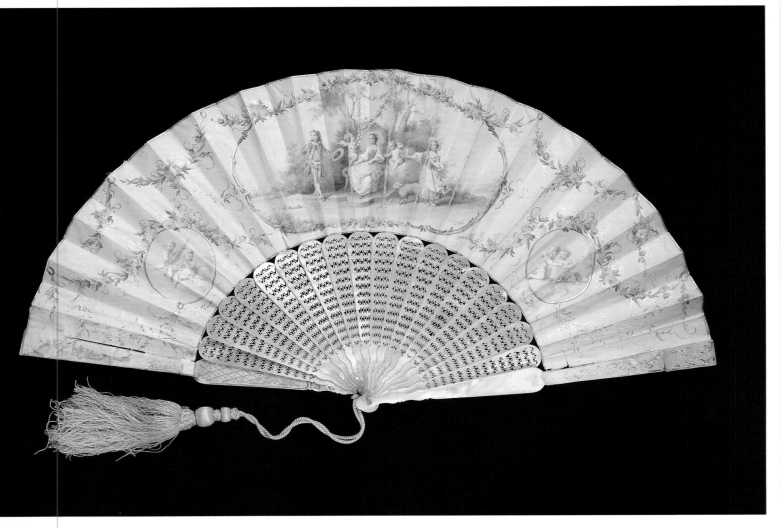

179. Back of the wedding fan.

and colorful impression (#130). Compared to Russian fans, the artistic impression left by this fan is more joyous and gay.

It is still difficult to say in which workshops and by which masters Russian fans of this period were created. But we can suppose that the conditions in which

Following pages:

181. Sheet of the fan made in black tulle. France, around 1880.

134

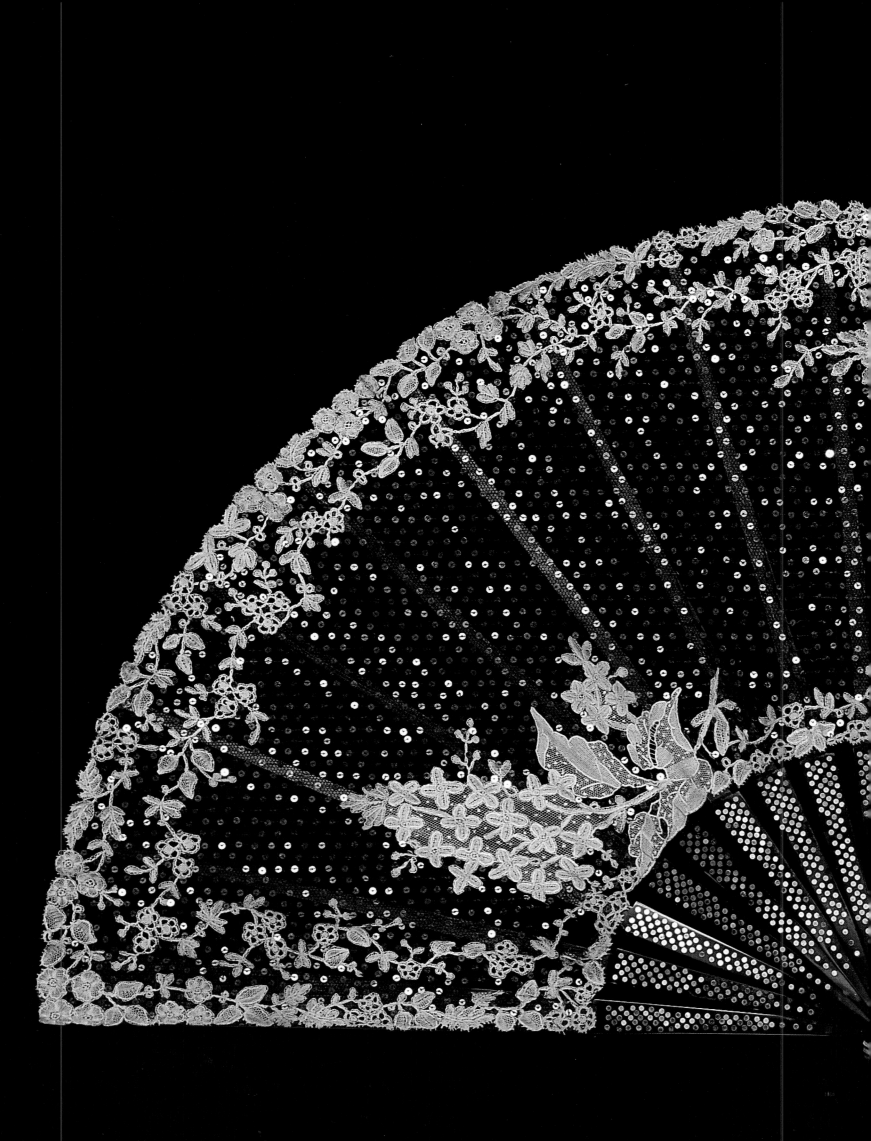

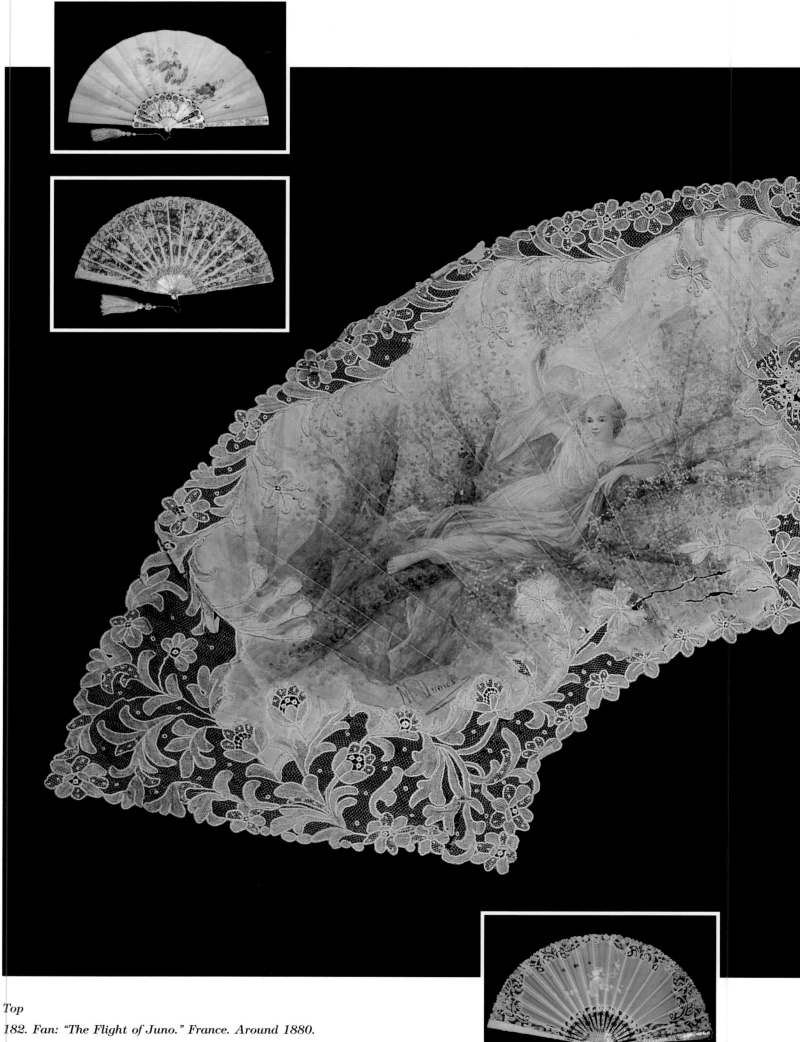

182. Fan: "The Flight of Juno." France. Around 1880.
183. Fan, with a lace sheet. France. Around 1880.

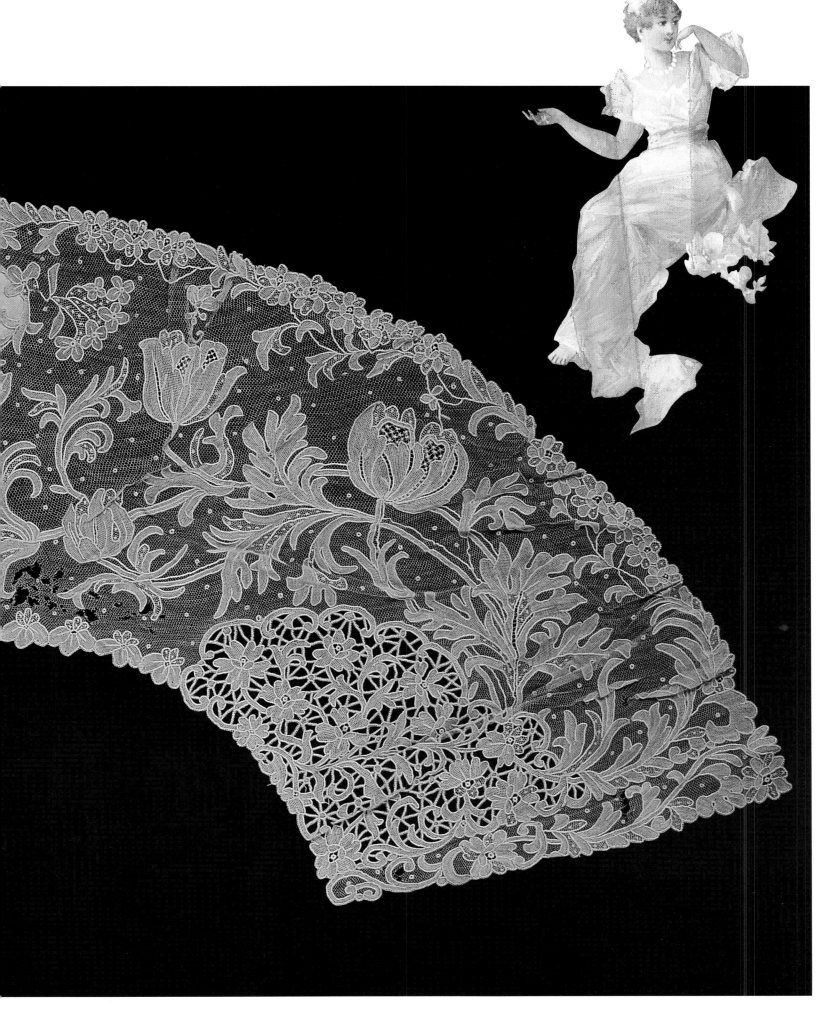

Bottom left

184. Lace fan, painted with silk.
France. Around 1880.

185. Sheet of the fan:
"Poucelina."
France. Around 1880.
And detail.

186. Jean-Auguste Dominique Ingres.
The Great Odalisque, 1814.
91 x 162 cm.
Musée du Louvre, Paris.

187. Fan with a sheet in painted silk.
France. Around 1880.

they were produced were the same as those at the end of the 18th century. I. N. Oukhanvona, researching the localization of master bone carvers, affirms that they, particularly those from Kholmogore, worked in the capitals, where they would spend short stays executing works on order[139]. This same study cites the example of a fan, created by a bone carver from Kholmogore in the 1820's, of eighteen blades in the shape of bowling pins painted in classical motifs[140]. The author affirms also that at the beginning of the 19th century, St. Petersburg became one of the centers of bone carving[141].

188. Jean-Auguste Dominique Ingres. The Slave Odalisque, 1839. Oil on canvas, 74.9 x 102.9 cm. Cambridge, Fogg Art Museum.

Fans conserved their small dimensions until 1827[142]. Then, following the evolution of fashion, which manifested itself in the feminine costume, they began little by little to grow larger and acquire a new appearance.

Romantic tendencies came to supplant sentimentalism in the 1830's, and continued until mid-century. In the fashion which spread to dress, it seems that during this period the tastes of the 18th century were reborn. Petticoats appeared, dresses were made of thick fabric in very rich tones. Something similar occurred in decorative art, where previous styles, characteristic to the 18th century were reborn, that is to say the "second empire baroque" made its appearance. Fans did not escape this general evolution of styles. In painting, representations of castles, knights and troubadours

189. Fan: "The Young Girl and the Doves." France. Around 1880.

appeared again, as well as oriental scenes. The decoration of fans was often produced in a retrospective spirit or, as we say now, in the style of "historicism." It suffices to observe a Russian fan of five cartels, probably

created in St. Petersburg, to get a feel for the romantic nostalgia for past centuries. This object was produced at the beginning of the 1830's, and it does not imitate sufficiently the 18th century, by which it was not really influenced. One senses a transition in the processes of decoration from classicism to something new. In ornamentation, the symmetric disposition of the cartels on the sheet, the ordered arrangement of motifs, the abundance of sequins and of blades representing figures of steel betray the use of past processes. But even in the nature of representation, in the appearance of characters, whether on the sheet or on the blades, in which are designed a group of fashionable people, we sense some romantic notes, some elements borrowed from the past. That is to say, the same traits which irrevocably become that style which is called "historicism" (#67).

The collection of the Museum of Ostankino has several fans from Western Europe, produced in the spirit of "historicism" (#'s 98, 100, 103, etc...). Of this type, the French fan "The Reception at the Lord's House" (#96) is very representative. The bone blades of the frame are executed in a fashion so archaic that one would take this specimen for a work of the 1760's. On the sheet, in the middle of a rich decorative frame, and occupying the entire surface, is a scene of a reception in a lord's

192. Fan with a two-sided sheet: "The Rendezvous in the Park." France. Around 1890.

Preceding pages:

190. Lace fan. France. Around 1880.

191. Fan: "Flora in a Chariot." France. Around 1880. And detail.

193. Fan: "Gallant Scene." France. Around 1890.

house, consisting of several characters and several phrases from a work of literature. All the characters, as well as the objects and the architecture which surrounds them, are taken from the 18th century. The objective of the producers of this work, which was to give an impression of antiquity or an old look, was a great

194. Two-sided fan:
"Gallant Scenes in the Park."
France. Around 1890.

195. Two-sided fan in the style of Art Nouveau.
France.
Border between the 19th and 20th centuries.

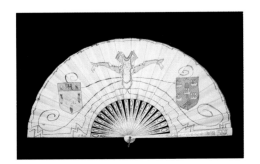

196. Back of the fan.

198. James McNeill Whistler
Symphony in White n°2
The Little White Girl, 1864.
Huile sur toile. 76,5 x 51,1 cm
Tate Gallery, Londres.

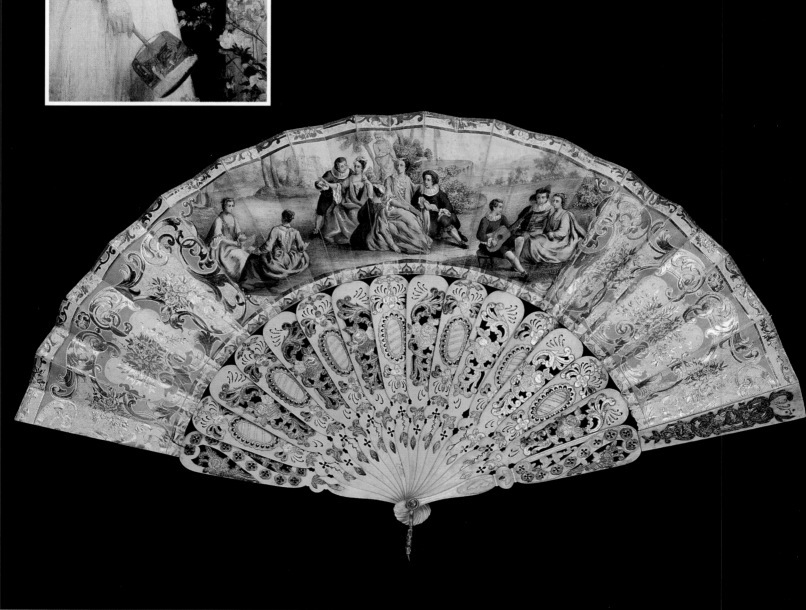

199. Eventail à deux faces :
« Groupe dans le parc ». Angleterre (?)
1850 - 1860.

success.

In the attempts to create a complete illusion of an antique, the masters of decorative art went so far that it is sometimes difficult to determine exactly the date at which an object was made. This applies to fans as well. This is the case, for example, of a German fan from the 1840's, "Gallant Scenes in a Park" (#122). The magnificently carved blades in mother-of-pearl, inlaid and carrying representations of landscape motifs, architectural edifices and figures of swans do not only recall but reproduce almost perfectly the creation of master carvers of the 18th century.

200. Back of the fan: "Gallant Scene."

The design of the sheet, with the motifs of flowers and framing plants, reproduces to such a degree the manner of decorating of the middle of the 18th century, that only a few details, barely perceptible in the costumes of the characters and the technique and arrangement of the decorative elements, enable the correct determination of the true period of its creation.

The themes of the painting of fan sheets of the second quarter of the 19th century were more varied.

Mythological subjects and antiques were still represented, as we see in the example of the French fans "The Victory of Amphitrite" (#105), "The Young

201. Two-sided fan: "Gallant Scene in the Park." Germany. Around 1840.

Sirens" (#97) and "The Young Girls on the Shore" (#104).

Some characters were inspired by literary prototypes. We can cite, for example, the French fans "The Reception at the Lord's House" (#96), already mentioned, "The Reception with the King" (#99), "Poucelina", etc.

Next to the enumerated motifs, all through the 19th century there continued to exist, in the designs of fans, conforming to sentimental tendencies which were already manifest, the theme of the gallant and idyllic pastoral, treated in a retrospective fashion, in the new spirit.

Examples of such include the German fan "Gallant Scenes in a Park" (#122) and those which are masterworks of Western Europe: "The Picque-Nique" (#131) and "The Concert" (#132).

It is necessary to note that in the 19th century, at the same time as fashionable costume, the fan entered little by little into the less aristocratic levels of society such as the merchants, the small bourgeoisie and the clergy. Around the middle of the century, the general democratic tendencies of the art of the period began to be reflected in the themes of fans. In place of pastoral images and of peasants and of the sentimental representation of morals and the life of common people, scenes of daily life, daily events and historical facts began to be depicted in a realistic manner. The collection of the Museum of

202. Back of the two-sided wedding fan. And detail.

Ostankino possesses many fans presenting such motifs. On one of the Italian fans (#125) is an episode of the wars between Italy and Austria. The painting of the two sided fan "The Bullfight" was done by a Spanish painter of the first order. One of the sides represents

150

203. Two-sided wedding
fan.
Italy. 1850-1860.

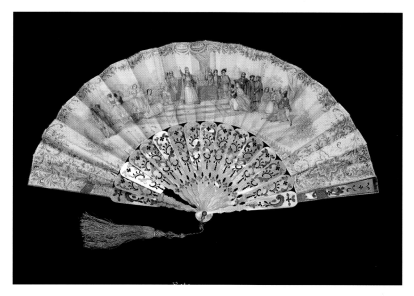

204. Two-sided fan:
"The Reception With the
Doge of Venice."
Italy. Middle of the 19th
century.

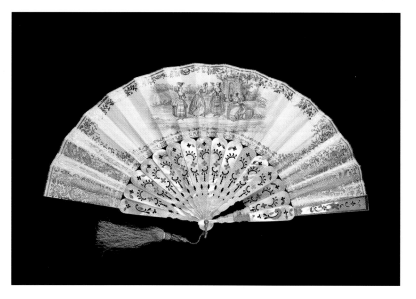

205. Back of the fan.

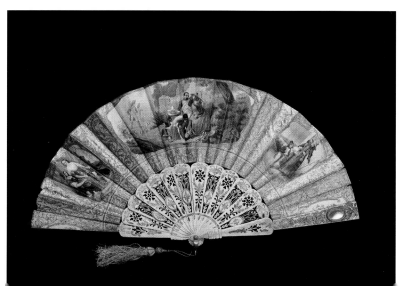

206. Two-sided fan with
three cartels.
Italy. Around 1860.

with brilliance and realism a festival with a flamenco dance at the centre and on the other side one sees the combat between two matadors and a bull. The talented production of the bone blades in openwork, presenting the motif of vines, (#127) attracts our attention.

The very lively sketch of the sheet of a Ukrainian fan, "The Rural Wedding" (#94), deserves attention. The author obviously observed daily life and reproduced, in democratic tradition, a marriage ceremony in the streets of a Ukrainian village, which was perhaps that of the owner of the fan, on the back of which is a coat of arms.

Near the middle of the 19th century, the reappearance of baroque traits in decorative and applied art, the changing of the cut and the increasing weight of women's dresses is reflected in the form and decoration of fans. Their dimensions grew considerably, their blades became massive and bare and for the fabrication of the sheets, thick fabrics decorated with paint and embroidery

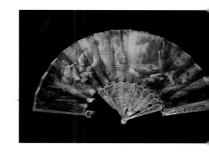

209. Fan:
"Gallant Scene with
some Lovers."
Spain. Around 1870.

came into use.

During the period we are describing, the fan became more and more linked to the feminine costume. It was often the object of a special order so as to go with a particular outfit for an important event. There are, for example, in the collection of the Museum of Ostankino

210. Back of the fan:
"The Bullfight."

153

two marriage fans of which one (#106) was, according to evidence, made to go with a wedding dress, which is seen in the nature of its design. This design, in pastel and joyous tones, occupies the entire sheet and represents the scene of the dressing of the bride before she is taken before the altar. This design was produced by the French fan painter Calamatta. The light colored, openwork blades, with a repeating crossed embroidery, are in mother-of-pearl and covered with gold. The surprisingly harmonious union of all the details, the great art with which the painting was produced, the brilliance of the elegant and glittering frame gives to the whole fan an air of celebration and a clear and joyous appearance.

In the second half of the 19th century, fan sheets in lace, guipure, satin and velvet appeared. It is necessary to note that the sheets in lace of Russian fans of this period, and even before, were prefabricated, specially braided or woven from separate remnants. The fans with lace sheets of the collection of the Museum of Ostankino (#'s 83, 84, 88, etc...) can bear witness to this. The fans made of feathers, certainly ostrich feathers, in the most varied tones, became very popular. Fans were very often made entirely of blades in shell, bone, or horn.

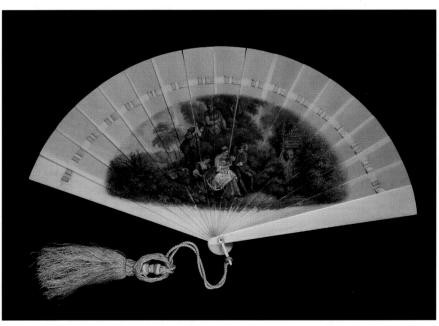

A fan in gray ostrich feathers and with blades in shell is particularly beautiful (#72).

On fans that were ordered to go with particular outfits or for the occasion of well defined events, it became the custom to write: the dates of these events, one's initials, coat of arms, monogram or a few words on

156

215. Two-sided fan:
"The Concert."
Western Europe. Middle of the 19th century.

216. Back of the fan.

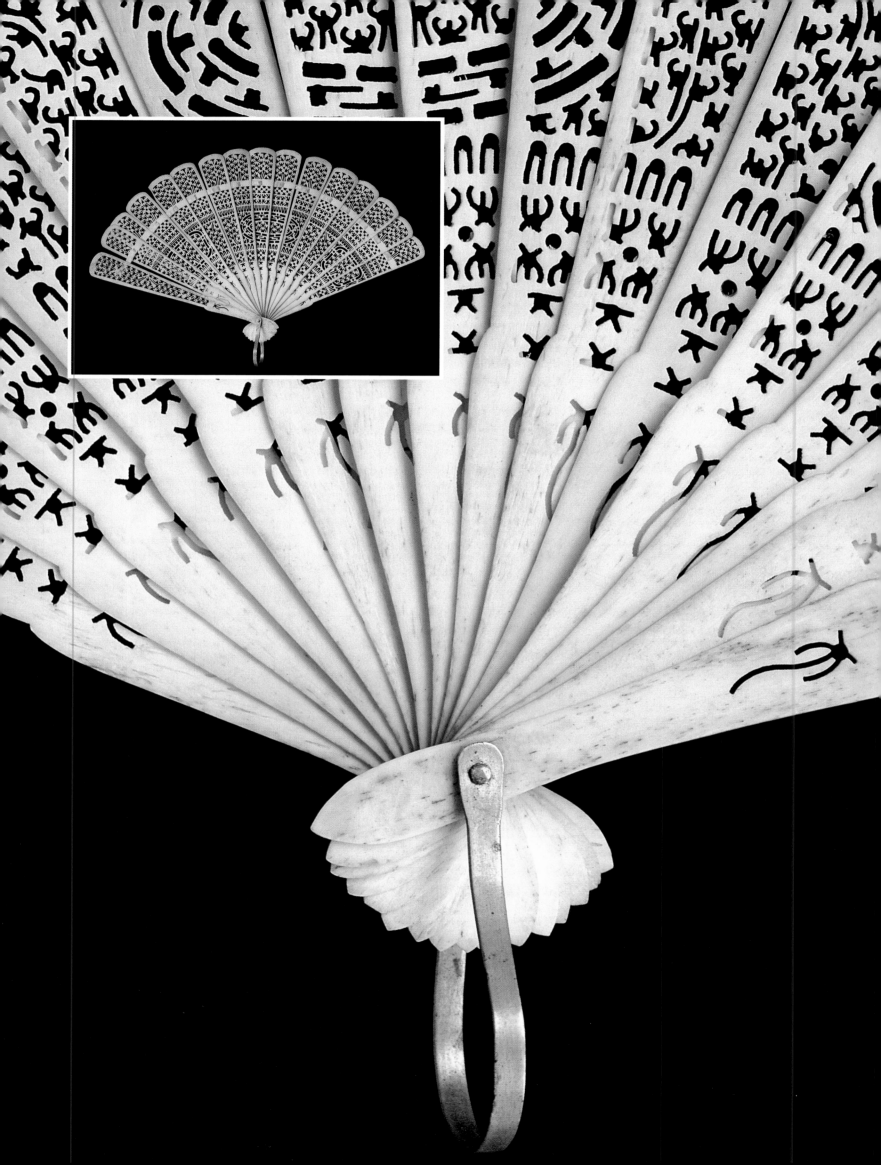

them before giving them.

On one of the lace fans of the collection of Ostankino, we can see a gold monogram and a crown of a count fixed on the panache which indicates that the object belonged to the countess A. A. Tatischeva (#88). This fan can be considered as an example of the use of new materials. The blades of the frame are made of cellulose, which marvelously imitate works in shell. The satin sheet of another Russian fan (#78) carries, at the edge of the decorative design, the inscription "remember."

During this period it became fashionable to create fans of gold, on which the blades, specially adapted to receive writing, could receive diverse souvenir inscriptions.

Such is the example of the album fan which belonged to the princess S. V. Volkonskaïa (#68). The sixteen large and close together blades are covered with inscriptions and maxims, phrases to the memory of an event, aphorisms with profiles of the authors of these maxims.

It is necessary to note that the fashion of these original albums continued all through the second half of the 19th century and into the beginning of the 20th. Thus, one of the issues of the newspaper "Solntse Rossii" ("The Sun of Russia") reproduced the gold album fan of the

218. The Grand Duchess Elisabeth Fedorovna. 1900.

219. Lace fan representing Cupids in the clouds. Russia. Beginning of the 20th century.

actrice N. L. Tiraspolskïa. This object carries the autographs of famous men of the Russian theatre. Among these, we can cite the names K. S. Stanislavski, M. N. Ermolova, G. N. Fedotova, and O. O. Sadovskaïa[143].

During this period curious objects "by system" were created in which were placed fans. For example, walking canes of which the top, like a case, would receive a fan. It appeared and unfolded when a special button was pressed or a lever pulled[144].

At the beginning of the 1870's, the feminine costume

Page to the left:

217. Fan with a frame in openwork bone.
Russia. Beginning of the 20th century.

went through considerable transformations. The large petticoats disappeared. The dress shrank and acquired forms which elongated the silhouette, thus recalling the clothing worn by women during the second half of the 18th century.

The fan was also touched by this evolution. Its form now came closer to what was characteristic during the baroque period. Its dimensions became considerably larger due to the elongation of the closely packed blades and by the enlargement of the band of the sheet. Examples of such are the Russian fans with sheets of silk (#69 and 70). Afterwards, the fan continued to get bigger. Around the 1880's, the sheet took on imposing proportions. It was often entirely painted, as in the manner of a canvas. The French fan "The Flight of Juno" (#109) is characteristic.

The dimensions acquired by fans made them more and more the objects of mockeries and caricatures in humor journals. For example, in the journal "Punch," in 1880, the immense size of fans, which, at the theatre, bothered spectators, were ridiculed[145]. These imposing dimensions lasted until 1895[146]. Then the fan began to get smaller, its shape recalling the fans of the end of the 18th century. And only the appearance, at the end of the 19th century, of a new style, the Art

220. Fan in the form of a pliable screen.
Russia. Beginning of the 20th century.

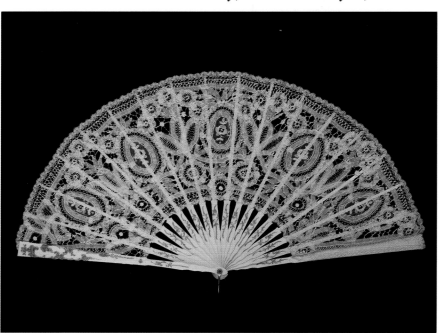

221. Lace fan.
Russia. Beginning of the 20th century.

Nouveau, generated a rich variety in the dimensions, form and decoration of the fan.

In the second half of the 19th century, with the democratization of the fan and its infiltration into the lower levels of society, we observe a tendency to lower the price. The sheets were simplified a little. They are often lacking in ornaments, made of simple fabrics and

Following pages:

224. Fan in black silk with lace.
Russia. Beginning of the 20th century.

160

222. *Case for a fan, with a bone chain and a charm.*

223. *The Grand Duchess Elisabeth Fedorovna. 1900.*

colored lace. The fashion journals published in Russia, the illustrated feminine reviews such as "Modnyi svet" ("The World of Fashion"), often proposed to direct the fabrication of fans to sheets woven in lace or cut from

Page to the left:

225. Fan in Japanese style representing chrysanthemums. Russia. Beginning of the 20th century.

226. Fan in satin, with a stitched representation of flowers and butterflies. Russia. Beginning of the 20th century.

227. Fan with a frame of engraved bone. Russia. Beginning of the 20th century.

228. Fan, in satin, representing branches of a flowering rosebush. Russia. Beginning of the 20th century.

cloth[147].

More accessible and less expensive materials were more and more often used: horn, cellulose, colored wood, cow bone. Moreover, the treatment and the ornamentation of the blades attempted to imitate more costly materials, such as: shell, mother-of-pearl, and ivory.

Examples of such include the fans made in Russia, of which one is of white ostrich feathers and has a frame of twenty blades in cellulose imitation shell (#91) and another, which represents Cupids, is mounted on blades of colored wood imitating ivory (#135).

At the end of the 19th century, gutta-percha was sometimes used to fabricate frames. This is seen in a fan in the form of a screen, comprised entirely of twenty blades in gutta-percha (#92). In the second half of the 19th century, it was mainly foreigners who held the monopoly of the fabrication and sale of fans in the large Russian cities, particularly in the capitals. Numerous advertisements published in the Russian newspapers document this.

"The English store of the house of commerce of the brothers A. and V. Salzfisch, situated in Moscow, Nikolskaïa Street, in the house of the Count Cheremetiev, offer fans in: ivory, shell, silk and wood, fashioned with a great elegance and in the new Parisian style"[148].

"The house of Y. Vizing offers fans of the new

style with a very large selection, from Paris. Perspective Nevski, house of Demidov, across from the Alexandrine Theater"[149].

This same situation is also seen in other cities. For example, in Kiev, the haberdashery and fashion store "Bristol" (Kiev, B. Vassilkovskaïa, #14) announced:

"Among other fashion articles, we offer a vast selection of fans"[150].

There were also, no doubt, Russian craftsmen and merchants, but it being that their names were drowned

out in the powerful chorus of foreign advertisements, they have not left any traces. But, among the numerous advertisements published in the "Bulletins" of the two capitals we discover, and exceptional fact, the following advertisement: "At the Slavic bazaar of the T. M. Matveev store, #1 and 3, we sell, among other articles, fans"[151].

229. Fan, with a sheet of black
silk, representing a rosebush,
flowers and a bird.
Russia. Beginning of the 20th
century.

230. Fan, in peacock feathers,
in Japanese style, with flowers
and birds.
Russia.
Beginning of the 20th century.

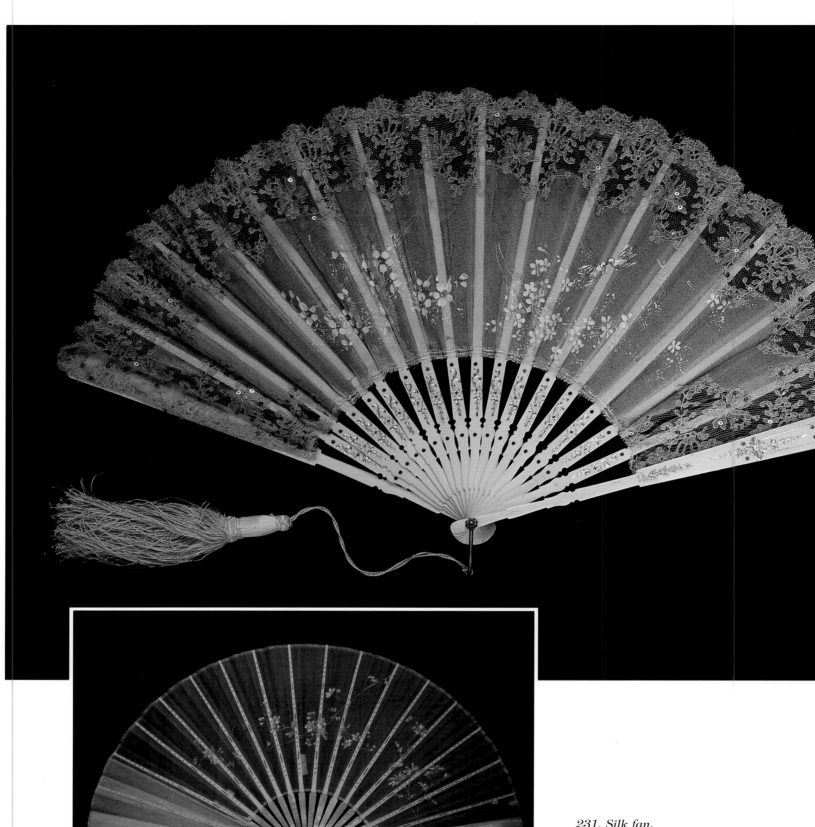

231. Silk fan.
Russia. Beginning of the 20th
century.

232. Fan with a silk sheet
representing two flowering branches.
Russia. Beginning of the 20th
century.

I. N. Oukhanova, in her book on master bone carvers, confirms that in the second half of the 19th century, Russian craftsmen were making and selling divers objects, fans among them. And she cites, as proof, a fan made in 1870 in chiseled bone accompanied by a case in the shape of a quiver[152]. The works of the collection of Ostankino confirm the participation of Russian masters in the creation of fans for the country.

When a series of fans from this period is attributed to someone, it is often difficult to set a very precise limit between the Russian models and those of Western Europe,

233. Fan with a frame in tortoise shell. Russia. Beginning of the 20th century.

234. Fan with a frame in carved bone with openwork embroidery. Russia. Beginning of the 20th century.

given the close links and commonalty of artist processes which lead to identical processes of decoration, not only in the decoration of fans but equally in other works of decorative art. Moreover, in the foreign owned workshops, worked Russian masters and Russian painters, who brought the traits of their own country to the works. This circumstance helped to discern the production of foreign firms, which worked in Russia, from the work of Russian masters.

This situation is particularly characteristic in the famous French company Alexandre. The producer, Alexandre, was the son-in-law of Desrochers, the owner of the famous fan house in Paris. Later he inherited the business[153]. He appeared in Russia in the 1860's selling very modestly, beginning a business. "Alexandre, turner and fabricator on the Perspective Nevski, is to be found between the small Morskaïa Street and the big Morskaïa Street, at #11, in the house of Stroubinski. Large selection and great variety of umbrellas of all types, the level of price of which goes from the very reasonable to the most elevated," announced the "Bulletin of St. Petersburg."

At the end of the 19th century – beginning of the 20th century, Alexandre was already the largest producer of fans. His house possessed subsidiaries: stores and workshops in Russia[154] as well as in other countries. The

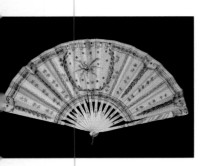

235. Fan, with a sheet in silk painted in the "Second Empire" style. Russia. Around 1910.

case of one of his fans carries a ticket with the inscription, "Alexandre. Fan maker to their majesties: the Empress of France, the Empress of Russia, the Queen of England, the Queen of Spain, 14, Boulevard Montmartre, Paris." Next to the large fan houses of France, such as Desrochers, Kees, Duvelleroy, this company manufactured

236. Fan with a sheet in painted silk, trimmed with down. Russia. Around 1910.

Following pages:

237. Fan with a sheet of black painted silk. France. Beginning of the 20th century.

170

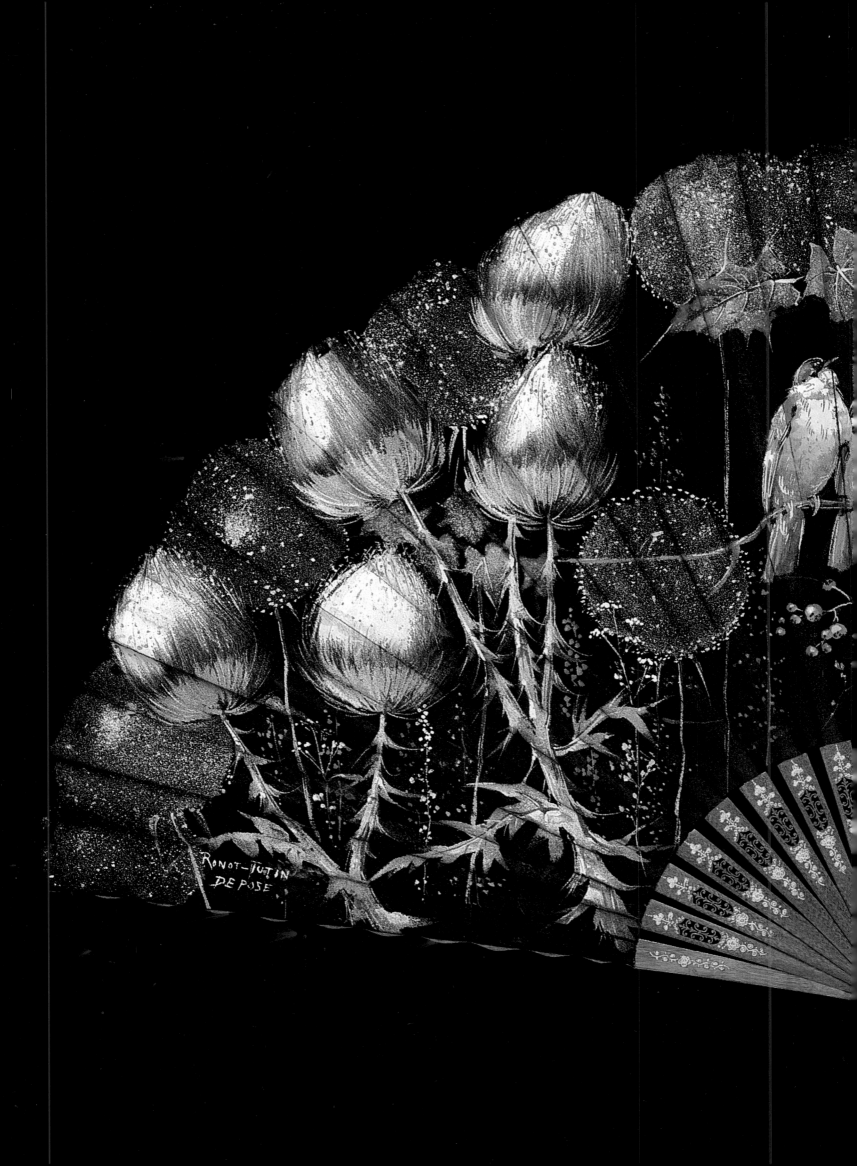

objects of marvelous quality of a very elevated artistic level because it employed painters and masters of talent. Mazé-Sencier enumerated a series of fans, figuring in the catalogue of the sale of the Alexandre firm, which took place in Paris in 1875. Among other manufacturers of fans are cited names of painters who we also find in the collection of the Museum of Ostankino: "J. Calamatta: 'Triumphant Venus' 1,360 francs; Donzel: 'The Wine Harvest' 136 francs; Picou: 'Spring' 250 francs"[155].

A fan, embroidered with sequins (#80), is an elegant example of the work of this company in St. Petersburg. Its frame, executed according to the traditions of the style proceeding the Art Nouveau, came from France but the sheet, the same as on the final assemblage, was produced in St. Petersburg.

In the second half of the 19th century, in Russia, an immense influx of fans from the West arrived, mostly from France, which became, during this period, the

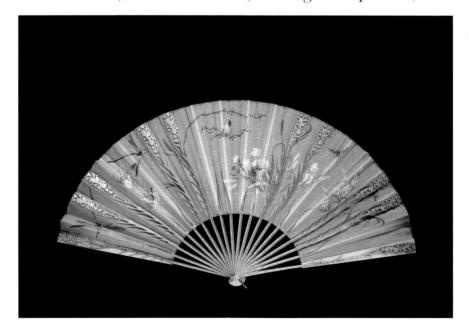

principle exporter of fans. The Great French Encyclopedia, of the end of the 19th century, indicates that around the 1880's, France exported eight million francs worth of fans per year[156].

In Russia too, fans coming from Paris, which during this period made the law in the domain of fashion, were particularly in demand. And certainly, the publicity concerning them aroused attention.

Even the names of the stores, in which fans were sold, were images of France. For example, "The City of Paris" in St. Petersburg[157] or the store "A la Toilette" in Moscow[158]. Until 1917, the stores of the French master Alexandre, situated at 11, Perspective Nevski, 10, Petrovka Street, as well as the stores of the Ralley company[159] of the tow cities and the store A. Mathieu on the Kouznetski Bridge in Moscow, which sold "wedding boxes and fans"[160], were very popular.

At the end of the 19th century – beginning of the 20th century, there was seen, in all art forms, a strong influence of the style in vogue during the period, the Art Nouveau. The characteristic traits of this style (the imitation of previous figuratives, a virtuoso stylization and interlacing of forms, as well as the principle of dynamic equilibrium) are also certainly reflected in the decoration of fans[161].

We can cite, for example, two Russian fans, the sheets of which have a form characteristic of Art Nouveau. The length, a little shortened, rounded by a sort of hump in the middle, they show a distancing vis à vis the traditional harmonious lines of the segments of the half circles. One of these fans was made in goose feathers, painted blue and fixed on blades of blue wood, bordered by a silver embroidery (#90). The broken form of the other fan, which presents flying birds in pastel tones, is accented by a light fluttering border of down (#150).

After 1908, we observe a tendency towards the augmentation of the size of fans. Their exceptional blades became more delicate, longer and, in their intentional simplicity, they give proof of a great study and elegance. They are often covered with fine engravings, expertly inlaid and painted in the new stylistic tendencies. The sheets are made of fine half transparent and translucent fabrics in very somber tones, as if they materialized the symbols of Art Nouveau: day and night. The design of the sheets was dominated by motifs of plants and flowers specific to the style in vogue.

Two beautiful French fans of magnificent design, in the spirit of the new style, were produced by the painter Tutin, with a great knowledge of the norms of the art of decorating fans. One of these represents, in an impressive manner, a cornucopia containing flowers (#153), which stands out on a dark background and the other, of birds surrounded by thistles and balls of white dandelions (#151).

A French fan, the sheet of which represents insects and birds among irises and roses, is itself also impressive. Its blades, in sculpted, gilded wood, were executed with talent in the Art Nouveau style and are presented in the form of winding stems with plumage and leaves at the ends (#152). This fan is even more interesting as it belonged to the grand-daughter of the famous Russian poet F. I. Tioutchev.

Paralleling the very distinct particularities of the new style, there also lived a good amount of romantic, oriental and classical traits in the decoration of fans, given that Art Nouveau had, as one of its properties, particularly

240. Fan with a painted black sheet. France. Beginning of the 20th century.

176

in its latter stages, the creative use previous periods.

Thus, in the 1910's, elements entered into vogue which seemed to be a rebirth of classicism, which took the name of neoclassicism or Second Empire. It is in the Second Empire style that one of the Russian fans (#149) was produced, of which the dimensions and design of the sheet recreate the fan models "Lilliputians" of the beginning of the 19th century. And only the rarefied blades of the frame differ from the forms of the Empire period.

An extremely impressive fan, created by the famous French master Duvelleroy[162] in the 1910's, also recalls by its dimensions and form, the fans of the beginning of the 19th century. To perfect the resemblance, its silk sheet, richly adorned with sequins and bordered with little fluttering feathers, carries an engraving reproducing a fashion drawing from the 1820's (#155).

Two Russian specimens executed in a manner to imitate Japanese fans, with a nearly "facsimile" reproduction of the design of the sheets and the manner of the sculpting of the frame. One of the two carries a brilliant design on white and the other flowers on a silk sheet mounted on blades of chiseled cyprus (#139).

A screen with seventeen blades in bone, imitating antique forms, was executed with whimsy and elegance. It fits in a case in the form of a dagger sheath covered with blue velvet. The finery of the case is enriched by a decorative chain in bone, with a charm and a hook in relief, permitting it to be suspended from the belt of a dress (#136).

Near the end of the 19th century, and at the beginning of the 20th, in the West as in Russia, fans in the form of old handle screens became popular again[163]. But their sheets were certainly fabricated with blades of bone, shell or in other hard materials, as for example, another specimen, made in Russia, at the beginning of the 20th century, in shell (#145).

It is certainly necessary to give some attention to a screen of the collection of the Museum of Ostankino, produced, it seems, in

241. Fan:
"The Rendezvous,"
with a sheet in
painted silk and
stitched with sequins.
France. Around 1910.

178

Spain in the 1910's, as a souvenir fan and even as an object of curiosity. Its fabric sheet can, with the help of a cord, come out of or fold into the handle, which serves the role of a case (#156).

The beginning of the 20th century marked the great vulgarization of fans and their future democratization, that is to say their infiltration into all levels of society, their use in popular festivals and their acquisition as souvenirs.

One of the French fans from end of the 19th century – beginning of the 20th century, which represents feminine costumes of the middle ages, was probably created for the occasion of a carnival festival (#121).

In the collection of the Museum of Ostankino is a souvenir fan conserved, the sheet of which is printed on both sides with a representation of Spanish bullfights. Such fans were often sold as souvenirs of famous bullfights.

Stores offered, as souvenirs, fans as small gifts to thousands of shoppers in Moscow. In the collection of the author is a simple paper fan of this type, which his mother received when, as a young girl, she made a small purchase at the Ostrooumov store. On the fan, written in gold, is the name of the store: A. M. Ostrooumov Company. Moscow.

The great democratization of fans, the specificity of their artistic image, generated a desire to collect them. Fraipont, in his book on the art of fan fabrication, cites the fact that the largest collection of fans in France was assembled by the owners of the fan making houses of Desrochers, Duvelleroy, and Alexandre. This collection consisted of 1,500 fans.

Fans struck the imagination of writers, inspiring poetic works. For example, N. N. Vrangel published an essay, "The Blood and the Fan," in which he depicts with originality, the coloring of Spain: "The Blood and the Fan: here are two words which describe all the spirit of Spain. Blood everywhere: in the prison confines of the Inquisition, in the macabre supplications, submitted to by Saints, represented in the paintings of church altars, blood in the Spanish sand, flooded with sunlight, of smiles and bright colors of dress. And in the

Following pages:

242. Fan presenting a fashion journal engraving. France. 1910-1920.

179

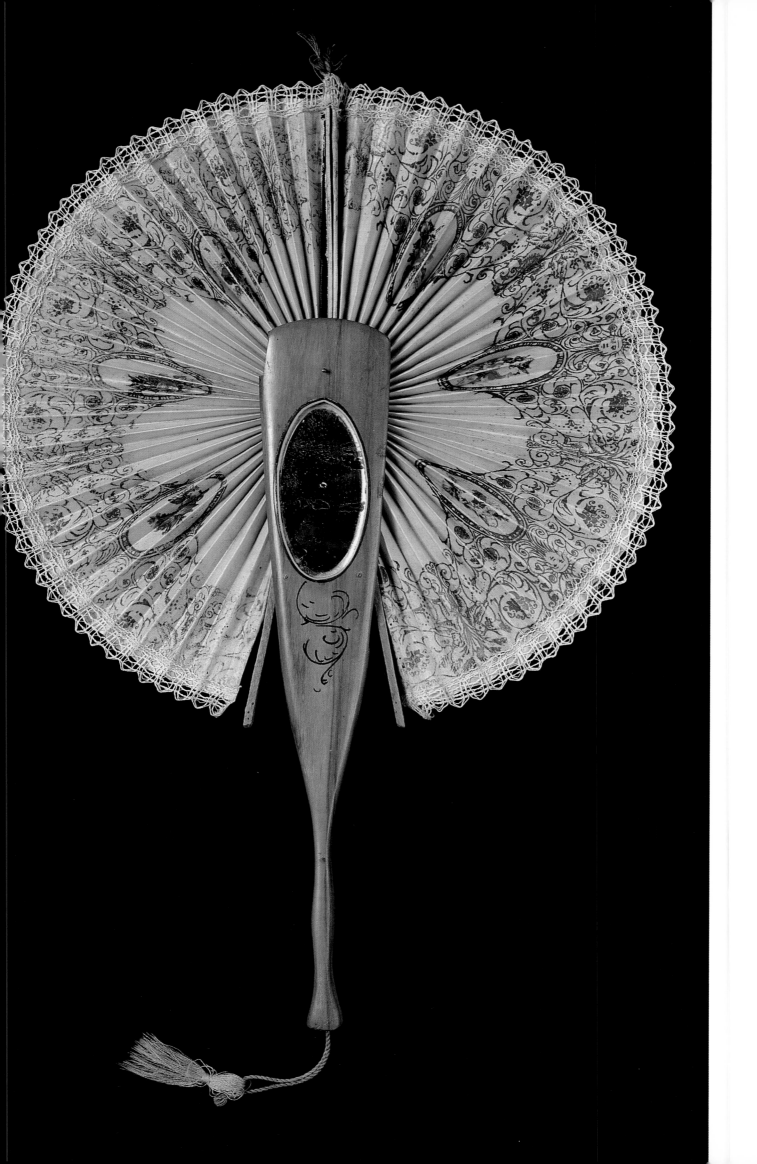

243. Fan with a handle-case.
Spain. Around 1910.

countryside (. . .)[164].

"And the fan, the instrument of malice and of affectation, the little fan, often black in sign of mourning, beats and trembles non-stop in the hand of all the women as if it was chasing away the spirit surrounding the word: blood. Everywhere in the streets and the houses, in the modest lodgment and in the pompous apartments, fans beat, as the pulse of life, in all of Spain. Such a flight of pigeons, which fly in flapping their wings, such malicious eyelashes, these little mechanical wings fan without end, directed by women (. . .)".

With time the rhythm of life changed; tastes modified. Numerous objects, living witnesses of the life and morals of past periods have disappeared. In Russia, the very important events which unfolded at the beginning of the 20th century and which brutally changed the way of life of Russian society contributed to this disappearance. The Russo-Japanese War and the First World War, the October Revolution, the upheaval of the social structure and of society life have taken from our lives numerous objects of former use. Among these is the fan, which used to play a considerable role in the life of humankind[165].

In our days, when the value of the fan as an historical monument, and its importance as a variety of decorative art have become evident, the study of the collection of museums has acquired a scientific, cognitive and practical interest.

*244. Johann
Friedrich August
Tischbein.
Portrait of Natalia
Saltikova, 1780.
Oil on canvas,
229 x 135 cm.*

245. Jean-Auguste Dominique Ingres. Madame Duvauçais, 1807. Oil on canvas, 76 x 59 cm. Chantilly, Musée Condé.

246. Jean-Auguste Dominique Ingres. The Baron James de Rothschild, 1844-1848. 141.8 x 101.5 cm. Collection Guy de Rothschild, Paris.

Press Chronicle of 1769-1790

Journal "Vsiakaïa Vsiatchina" ("Concerning Everything"). 1769, #9, p. 373-374.

". . . Yesterday, I participated in a conversation which enabled me to see a very beautiful woman. She was very sure of her beauty and she endeavored, by all methods, to make us notice it and attract all looks towards her. She found a reason to carry her regard towards the heavens, so that one could remark how beautiful her eyes were in that position. Then, point-blank, she held out her arm and asked, "Who is behind the door?" Which meant "Admire the whiteness of my hand." After which she dropped her fan and, lowering herself to pick it up, she showed her breasts a little more than usual. In picking up the fan she lifted her skirt a little so that one could see her cute little feet, which had the honor of carrying her. A little later, she left her seat, began to laugh, completely opening her lips; we know that she wanted us to admire her teeth."

The Satirical Journal, 4th Edition, 1790, p. 101-102.

"An energetic young girl, capable of always keeping her body fit, and who for this reason seems lively and her breasts made up with make-up, with difficult respiration, and who knows how to flutter her fan and to skillfully use it to cool herself and blow her hair (. . .) due to these great qualities (. . .) marries a young man possessing 1,500 souls."

The Satirical Journal, p. 20-22.

"In this city, fashions have attained such a level of perfection that they have been transformed into a regulated science. Some sticks or pieces of bone, united by some taffeta or by a picture glued on them, have become so important in the hands of the beautiful sex, that women, with the aid of these toys, are capable of expressing diverse: sentiments, desires, parables, malices, feigned severity, etc. These sticks are, for the faces of these belles, a sort of movable fence. This little fence must above all hide their faces when a yawn or a flash of laughter opens their mouths so wide, that one can see teeth or the sky itself inside. Upon seeing something inconvenient or when one hears ambiguous words, this little movable fence puts itself so deftly in front of the eyes that, in hiding from them, it does not at all prevent to see or hear. When the pains of the heart make for biting of the lips and the gnawing of the fingernails, this little mobile shield makes it a duty to hide these gestures, as it renders invisible, the pallor or the blush, which covers the lovely little faces of the belles when they are angry, envious, or full of shame. The weaker sex has also attributed to these sticks the function of a wind making machine."

247. Fashion engraving from the journal, "Parisian Fashions. Office of Historic Fashions and Costumes." 1803.

The Satirical Journal, p. 26-28.

Fans also serve as secret letters, because today, in pretending to be amiable and polite, one asks his beloved permission to write on her fan, as an impromptu, some tender lines or a completely different declaration of love. It often happens that the belle, under the influence of written verse, writes something in her turn, as by accident, and this message, during the next encounter, shall be taken by the impatient admirer as the answer to his own lines and to his secret declaration of love. In a word, one can say that the goddess of love herself inspired human beings to invent these magic sticks, the use of which became acceptable and truly constitutes the secret science of belles and dandys."

Journal "Smes" ("Mix"), 1769 (quoted according to Verechtchaguine V. "The Fan and Grace." p. 90)

"Women, who know the world know, with their fans, how to express diverse passions: jealousy, in holding the fan close to their mouths, and without saying a word; indecent curiosity, while still preserving prudence, hide their faces with the open fan and observe through the blade of the frame that which would be embarrassing to look at with the naked eye. And love plays with the fan, as babies with toys, and makes of it all that which pleases him."

248. K. Kourts. Portrait of M. A. Cherbatova, 1855. Lithograph. Palace of Ostankino in Moscow.

249. Jean-Auguste Dominique Ingres. Madame Moitessier, 1852-1856. 120 x 92 cm. National Gallery, London.

250. James McNeil Whistler.
*The Princess of the Country of
Porcelain, 1863-1864.*
199.9 x 116 cm.
*Freer Gallery of Art,
Washington DC.*

GLOSSARY

Fan: instrument designed to obtain coolness, consisting of a frame and a sheet assembled in such a way that they can be unfolded in a closed band and deployed (opened) forming something with width, resembling the leaf of a tree, to serve as one has need of it (to fan oneself).

Screen: instrument designed to obtain coolness, composed of a flat sheet, of varying form, fixed to a handle.

Sheet: the upper part of a fan or screen. Presenting itself in the form of an elongated band, fixed to the blades of the frame (as a fan) or left as a sort of leaf, fixed to a handle (as a screen). Made of diverse materials: paper, cardboard, parchment, leather, cloth, feathers, etc. . .

Frame: the assembly of the blades of the fan, constituted of panaches, from the throat, which serves to support, and the ends (sometimes lacking in decoration), which are mounted and fixed at their inferior extremities by a rivet.

Blades: fine flat sticks, made of diverse materials (wood, bone, mother-of-pearl, metal) serving to hold the sheet of the fan in its upper part. Entirely chiseled blades exist, the lower portion of which is generally more elegant, and the upper portion, onto which the sheet is directly fixed, more simple. The blades are composed of the neck, executed in a more artistic manner, and the ends, more modest and narrow, which are attached together, on which the sheet is fixed. The panaches are larger and generally richly ornamented. They encase the fan on both sides, when it is closed.

Handle: pole on the upper part, of which is fixed the sheet of a screen.

Rivet: small nail (usually metal) serving to attach together, in a mobile manner, on their lower ends, the blades of the frame. Often decorated with stones on each side, as well as other materials. A ram is attached to the rivet, to permit the passage of a strap, often prepared with knots and tassels and serving to carry the fan in the hand or suspended from a belt.

251. James McNeil Whistler.
Red and Black.
The Fan, 1890's.
187.4 x 89.8 cm.
Hunterian Art Gallery, Glasgow.

EXHIBITION
CATALOGUES

**Catalogue of the exhibition of
1956.**
Catalogue of the exhibition of fans
organized at the Palace of
Ostankino in 1956 (coming from
the private collection of F. E.
Vichnevski). Moscow, 1956. Author
of the preface and of the contents:
N. A. Elizarova.

**Catalogue of the exhibition of
1980.**
Works of figurative and applied art
acquired in the last years at the
Palace of Ostankino among the
works of serf artisans. Catalogue of
the exhibition. Moscow, 1980.
(Author of the preface and of the
contents: A. F. Tcherviakov).

Album "Ostankino"
Art of serf artisans at the Palace of
Ostankino. Album. Leningrad,
1982. (group of authors).

**Catalogue of the exhibition of
1985.**
Exhibition "The Fans of the 18th
Century to the 20th Century –
Collection of the Palace of
Ostankino. Art of Serf Artisans."
Catalogue, Moscow, 1985. (Author
of the preface and of the contents:
A. F. Tcherviakov).

**Catalogue of the exhibition of
1987.**
Russia-France. The Age of the
Enlightenment. Franco-Russian
cultural relations in the 18th
Century. Catalogue of the
exhibition. Leningrad, 1987. (group
of authors).

*The following catalogue is divided
into three parts: the 18th, the 19th,
and the 20th centuries.*

*In each part, the objects are
grouped according to country. (The
numbers in parentheses correspond
to the numbers of the legends in
this work.)*

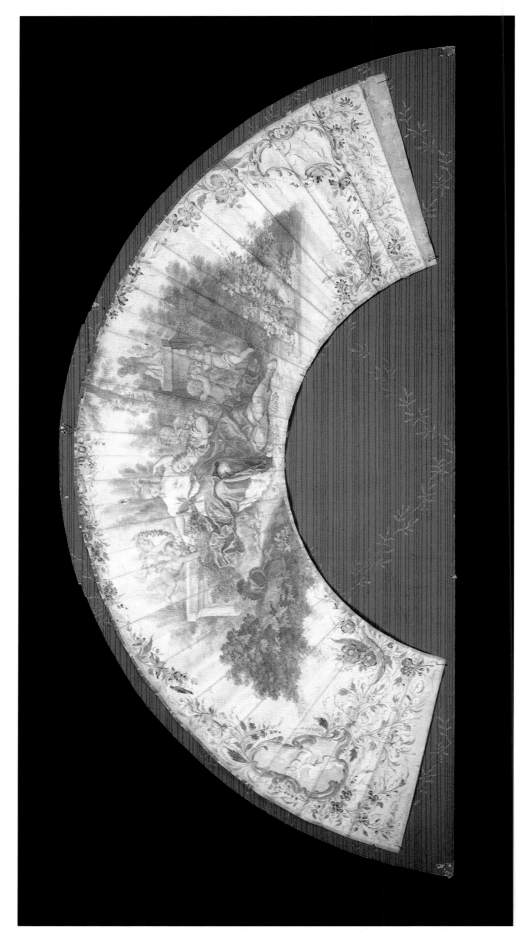

CATALOGUE

18TH CENTURY

RUSSIA

1 (30, 31). Two-sided fan with three painted cartels. Frame with 23 openwork bone blades.
Russia. Around 1750.
Paper, bone, taffeta, paint, sculpture, weaving, gilding.
38 x 65 cm.
Gift of F. E. Vichnevski in 1958.
9207/Pz-180

The three cartels on one side of the paper sheet carry painted representations: the personification of the three elements: Air, Earth and Water. In the left cartel, an allegory of Air is found: the skies symbolize all that is heavenly, divine, which is confirmed in the allegorical figures of Minerva, Juno and Zephyrus, situated on clouds. In the central cartel, an allegory of Earth is represented, in its daily life as it were (a scene of daily life: some children collecting the fruit of an apple tree). In the right cartel, an allegory of Water is found. On an immense stretch of sea, symbolizing the infinity of thought, small figures of two dreamers on the shore are represented. On the other side of the sheet we see a pastoral scene near an obelisk. The blades carry a chiseled design in rocaille set on a background of blue taffeta.

Documentation: Catalogue of the exhibition of 1956, #1. Album "Ostankino." Catalogue of the Exhibition of 1985, #1.

2 (33). Two-sided sheet of the fan "Renaud and Armidia."
Russia. Beginning of the 18th Century.
Parchment, paint.
14.5 x 55 cm.
Gift of F. E. Vichnevski in 1958.
9254/Pz-227

The parchment sheet represents a rendezvous scene in the gardens of the sorceress Armidia between the characters of the poem by Torquato Tasso: "Jerusalem Liberated." The knight Renaud is half lying against the seated Armidia and he holds in his right hand a mirror. To the left, at the feet of Armidia, is found the shield, the sword and the helmet thrown away by the knight. Five Cupids crown the lovers with flowers. The scene is framed with motifs of flowers and at the edges of the sheet are found two rocaille cartouches, of which each carries two cherubs. On the back is represented a couple of lovers in a park.

Documentation: Catalogue of the exhibition of 1956, #48. Album "Ostankino." Catalogue of the exhibition of 1985, #2.

3 (34). Two-sided fan with three cartels: "The Rendezvous in the Park." Frame of 14 bone blades.
Russia. 1770-1780.
Parchment, bone, painting, sculpture, engraving, inlaying, gilding.
28.5 x 51 cm.
Gift of F. E. Vichnevski in 1958.
9212/Pz-185

In the central cartel on the back of the parchment sheet a knight facing a seated lady is represented. In the side cartels are still-life drawings of fruit. On the other side, in a small medallion, kissing doves are found.

Documentation: Catalogue of the exhibition of 1956, #6. Album "Ostankino." Catalogue of the exhibition of 1985, #3.

4 (36). Fan with three cartels: "Knight with a Lady in the Park." Frame with 14 bone blades.
Russia. Around 1780.
Paper, bone, painting, sculpture, engraving, inlaying.
28 x 53 cm.
Gift of F. E. Vichnevski in 1958.

In the central cartel a couple of lovers near a fountain and a small boy bringing them a basket of flowers are represented. On the side cartels, we see rendezvous scenes in the pavilions of the park.

Documentation: Catalogue of the exhibition of 1956, #5. Album "Ostankino." Catalogue of the exhibition of 1985, #4.

5 (35). Two-sided fan with five cartels: "Rebecca at the Well." Frame with 14 bone blades.
Russia. Around 1870.
Parchment, bone, painting, sculpting, silver.
27.5 x 49 cm.
Gift of F. E. Vichnevski in 1958.
9213/Pz-186

In the central cartel a biblical scene is represented: the meeting, before a well, of Rebecca and the servant of Abraham. In the oval cartels situated on each side, to the right and left, are landscape drawings consisting of figures; two small cartels present a sheep and a box. On the other side of the sheet we see a bouquet of flowers.

Documentation: Catalogue of the exhibition of 1956, #7. Album "Ostankino." Catalogue of the exhibition of 1985, #5.

6 (37). Fireplace screen.
Russia. End of the 18th century – beginning of the 19th century.
Cardboard, wood, painting, gilding, turned engraving.
40 x 25 cm.
From The Hermitage Museum.
8720/Pz-14

On the cardboard sheet, in the framing of oak branches, a young girl is represented carrying a basket, walking on a road.

Documentation: Album "Ostankino." Catalogue of the exhibition of 1985, #6.

7 (2). Fireplace screen.
Russia. End of the 18th century – beginning of the 19th century.
Cardboard, wood, painting, gilding, turned engraving.
40 x 25 cm.
Arrived in 1936 from The Hermitage Museum.
8721/Pz-15

On the cardboard sheet, in a framing of oak branches, a young man is represented with a dog on the small dike of a village.

Documentation: Catalogue of the

FRANCE

8 (39). Two-sided fan sheet: "Games in the Park."
France. Middle of the 18th century.
Paper, painting.
15 x 56 cm.
Gift of F. E. Vichnevski in 1958.
9255/Pz-228

In a park, in the greenery, a group composed of young girls is represented and two young boys playing, with a knight in the centre. To the left on a bench is written in difficult to decipher script: Crevoisy (?). On the back we see three Cupids on clouds.

Documentation: Catalogue of the exhibition of 1956, #49. Catalogue of the exhibition of 1985, #8.

9 (40). Two-sided fan representing a pastoral scene. Frame with 19 mother-of-pearl blades.
France. Around 1740.
Paper, mother-of-pearl, gilded sheet, metal, painting, engraving, inlaying.
26.5 x 50 cm.
Acquired in 1978 by F. E. Vichnevski.
10812/Pz-280

On one side of the paper sheet a group of young peasants is represented, made up of four girls and of four boys who hold each other on the bank of a stream not far from the ruins of a brick wall. Near the stream are also found two dogs and five sheep. One young girl, standing to the left, is spinning wool with the aid of a distaff.. In the distance, we see a landscape with a village and a castle. On the other side, a scene of bygone life is presented. The openwork design in rocaille of the mother-of-pearl blades consists of figures of cherubs, of ladies and of knights.

10 (41). Two-sided fan representing a scene of a rural festival. Frame with 21 mother-of-pearl blades.
France. Around 1760.
Parchment, mother-of-pearl, silver and gold sheet, painting, engraving, inlaying.
29.5 x 51 cm.
Acquired in 1978 by F. E. Vichnevski.
10811/Pz-282

One side of the parchment sheet represents some scenes of a rural festival. In the centre, a group of villagers watch a representation of a theater of marionettes. To the right, we see a dance around an organ. To the left, we see a woman explaining to three children the mechanism of a sun dial. On the other side two cherubs are represented on the balcony of a pavilion of the park in rocaille: one of them holds a fan, the other watches through a telescope. On the blades of the frame, three rocaille cartouches carry the indented figures of lovers and of cherubs; the panaches present Ethiopian figures.

Documentation: Catalogue of the exhibition of 1985, #10.

11 (42,43). Two-sided fan: "The Birth of Venus." Frame with 15 shell blades.
France. Around 1760.
Paper, shell, painting, sculpting, engraving, gold sheet inlaying.
28.5 x 54 cm.
Gift of F. E. Vichnevski in 1958.
9215/Pz-188

In the centre of the sheet some Tritons are represented holding a shell, in which Venus is found. Some Cupids fly above them. To the left, some nymphs and Tritons sail on dolphins. To the right, a water genie watches from behind a rock, below which swims a siren. On the other side, we see a rocky island in a watery element without limit with a sail in the distance. In

the upper right the stamp of the customs port of St. Petersburg is affixed. In the openwork ovals of the frame, the same as in the mesh blades and in the form of a column, are indented some figures of ladies, knights, cherubs as well as some birds and flowers.

Documentation: Catalogue of the exhibition of 1956, #9. Catalogue of the exhibition of 1985, #4.

12 (44). Fan: "Abigail Facing David." Frame with 20 mother-of-pearl blades.
France. Around 1759.
Parchment, mother-of-pearl, gold and silver sheet, painting, sculpting, inlaying.
29 x 54.3 cm.
Gift of F. E. Vichnevski in 1958.
9216/Pz-189

The parchment sheet reproduces a scene of biblical legends. Abigail is the wife of Nabal, the rich tribal chief. To avoid that her husband, who had refused his aid to David, sees all his goods pillaged, she comes on her knees to offer some bread, wine and other presents to the future king and his soldiers.

On the other side, the stamp of the customs port of St. Petersburg is affixed with the date: 1759. The blades carry the indented figures of ladies and cherubs and the panaches of helmeted soldiers.

Documentation: Catalogue of the exhibition of 1956, #10.

13 (45). Fan: "The Bird Catchers in Love." Frame with 15 inlaid bone blades.
France. Around 1770.
Silk, bone, sequins, painting, sculpting, embroidery, gilding, inlaying.
28.5 x 53 cm.

Gift of F. E. Vichnevski in 1958.
9218/Pz-191

Framed with a bicolor ribbon and colored garlands, a couple of lovers catch birds with snares.

Documentation: Catalogue of the exhibition of 1956, #12. Album "Ostankino." Catalogue of the exhibition of 1985, #12.

14 (46). Two-sided fan: "The Pastoral." Frame with 14 mother-of-pearl blades.
France. 1770-1780.
Paper, mother-of-pearl, sequins, gold and silver sheet, painting, sculpting, embroidery, inlaying.
27.5 x 50 cm.
Gift of F. E. Vichnevski in 1958.
9221/Pz-194

One side of the sheet represents, in the centre, the rendezvous of a young couple, and to the right a child watches them from behind a hillock. On each side, to the right and left, we see representations of theater accessories and of pigeons. All the drawn subjects are framed with garlands of flowers. On the other side, motifs of flowers are disseminated. The blades carry the silhouettes of ladies, of Cupids and flowers inlaid with metal leaf.

Documentation: Catalogue of the exhibition of 1956, #15.

15 (47). Fan: "Family Love." Frame with 13 bone blades.
France. 1770-1780.
Author: monogrammer C.N.
Silk, paper, bone, sequins, metallic thread, painting, sculpting, engraving, embroidery, gilding.
28 x 49 cm.
Gift of F. E. Vichnevski in 1958.
9220/Pz-193

The central cartel of the silk sheet reproduces the famous painting by Jean-Baptiste Greuze: "The

Paralytic Served by His Children," painted in 1763 and which is today found in The Hermitage Museum. The left cartel represents a lute and a partition placed on a pedestal. The right cartel shows flowers in a vase in the form of an urn. The cartels are framed by a gold thread and abundant sequins. There is a signature in the form of a monogram: C. N. On the panaches are indented lyres and crossed torches.

Documentation: Catalogue of the exhibition of 1956, #14. Catalogue of the exhibition of 1985, #13.

16 (48). Two-sided fan: "The Altar of Love." Frame with 15 mother-of-pearl blades.
France. 1770-1780.
Silk, mother-of-pearl, sequins, gold and silver leaf, painting, sculpting, embroidery, inlaying.
28 x 52 cm.
Gift of F. E. Vichnevski in 1958.
9219/Pz-192

On one side, framed with gold and silver sequins, is found, in the central cartel: a knight, and four ladies walking in a park, as well as Cupid near the altar and two

peasants. The left cartel represents a seated lady, the right cartel: a knight leaning against a branch. On the other side, some small bouquets are drawn in three cartels and the stamp of the customs port of St. Petersburg is affixed. On the panaches figures of knights are engraved.

Documentation: Catalogue of the exhibition of 1956, #13. Catalogue of the exhibition of 1985, #14.

17 (49) Fan with three painted cartels. Frame with 16 shell blades.
France. 1770-1780.
Silk, shell, bone, sequins, painting, sculpting, embroidery.

27.5 x 49 cm.
Acquired in 1985 by K. V. Kouvyrdine.
11445/Pz-361

The central cartel represents a group of five people in front of the altar with Cupid. The side cartels show landscapes with flying balloons.

18 (50). Fan representing a group of musicians. Frame with 16 bone blades.
France. Around 1780.
Paper, silk, bone, sequins, sculpture, embroidery, engraving, silver, inlaying.
27.5 x 51.5 cm.
Gift of F. E. Vichnevski in 1970.
9685/Pz-267.

The central cartel represents a group of three characters. In the centre is seated a lady playing a lute. To the right, a knight holds a partition. To the left, a standing lady holds a basket containing flowers. At her feet is a little sleeping white dog.

19 (13, 51). Fan with three cartels: "The Rendezvous." Frame with 17 bone blades.
Painting by Kahenn.
France. Around 1780.
Silk, bone, metal, paste, sequins, gold thread, sculpture, embroidery, engraving.
21.7 x 41 cm.
Acquired in 1975.
10048/Pz-271

The central cartel represents a

couple of lovers half reclining on the ground. The side cartels show landscapes. The framing of the cartels and the whole of the sheet's surface is abundantly set with ornamental motifs and flowers, embroidered in silk, of sequins, of gold thread and of tulle mesh. The blades engraved with an elegant design are painted in gold and their upper parts, in the form of vases, carry small multicolored bouquets. The central cartel carries the signature to the left: Kahenn.

20 (53). Two-sided fan with five cartels: "What Says the Knight?" Frame with 16 bone blades.
France. Around 1780.
Silk, bone, lace, sequins, painting, sculpture, weaving, embroidery, inlaying.
30 x 53 cm.
Gift of E. V. Goldinger in 1949.
9169/Pz-175

The subject of the painting of the central cartel is borrowed from the engraving by N. Delaunay "What Says the Abbot?" In the centre, a lady is seated near a washstand. She questions a knight while pointing at a fabric she is offering him. On the right, in a chair, a musician is seated with his instrument. On the wall we can read the inscription: "What Says the Knight?" In contrast with the painting by Delaunay, in the drawing of the fan, the figure of the abbot is replaced by a

socialite, which lightens the subject a little. In the two round cartels, the technique of the engraving on silk represents scenes of antiquity. There are vases on the edges of the cartels. In the upper part, the sheet is bordered with lace from Alançon. All the cartels are framed with gold sequins. On the other side three modest bouquets are drawn and the stamp of the customs port of Riga is affixed.

Documentation: Album "Ostankino."

21 (52). Two-sided fan representing a pastoral scene. Frame with 14 mother-of-pearl blades.

France. Around 1770.
Paper, bone, mother-of-pearl, sculpture, gilding.
27.5 x 50 cm.
Gift of F. E. Vichnevski in 1958.
9217/Pz-190

One side of the sheet represents a pastoral scene: a group composed of three young girls, a child and a young man holding in his hand a wreath, is placed in the shadow of an oak. On the right, next to them, a goat is found. To the left, a little further away, is a small boy fishing. On the other side, we see a stylized landscape. The blades represent ladies, knights, Cupids, and other motifs and are inlaid with gold and silver leaf.

22 (54). Theater screen: "Blaise and Babette."
France. End of the 18th century.
Paper, cardboard, wood, engraving, painting, printing, turned engraving.
47 x 24 cm.
Acquired by I. V. and V. P. Cheremetiev in 1979.
10886/Pz-288

One side of the sheet represents a scene from the opera by N. Dezèze "Blaise and Babette," surrounded by drawings of flowers and accessories of the theater. On the other side an extract from the play is painted, headed by the inscription : "Blaise and Babette, comédie." Below there is the inscription: "A Paris chez Petit. Rue du Petit Pont à l'Image Notre Dame, #12." It is believed that in the 18th century this screen was in the theater of the Palace of Ostankino.

Documentation: Catalogue of the exhibition of 1980, #63. Catalogue of the exhibition of 1987, #685.

23 (55, 56). Theater screen: "The Marriage of Figaro."
France. End of the 18th century.
Paper, cardboard, wood, engraving, painting, printing, turned engraving.
46.5 x 24.5 cm.
Acquired by I. V. and V. P. Cheremetiev in 1979.
10889/Pz-291

One side of the sheet represents a scene from the theater, surrounded by drawings of flowers and theater accessories. On the other side there is a painted engraving: the notes of anarietta in a fashioned frame. Above there is the inscription: "Vaudeville of the Marriage of Figaro." And below: "A Paris chez Petit. Rue du Petit Pont à l'Image Notre Dame, #12." The composition is inspired by illustrations in the 1785 edition of the Marriage of Figaro drawn by Saint Quentin and conserved in the library of the Comédie Française (Henri Cohen H. Books of Engravings of the 18th Century. 1912, p. 125). It is believed that in the 18th century this screen was in the theater of the Palace of Ostankino.

Documentation: Catalogue of the exhibition of 1980, #65. Catalogue of the exhibition of 1987, #696.

24 (57). Theater screen: "The Right of the Lord."
France. End of the 18th century.
Paper, cardboard, wood, engraving, painting, printing, turned engraving.
45 x 23 cm.
Among a number of acquisitions from the 1920's.
2111/Pz-2

One side of the sheet represents an engagement scene surrounded by drawings of flowers and theater accessories. The other side reproduces a dialogue of the heroes of the play and one can read a little typographical inscription: "A Paris chez Petit. Rue du Petit Pont à l'Image Notre Dame. Grav. A Paris chez Petit."

Documentation: Album "Ostankino." Catalogue of the exhibition of 1985, #15.

25 (58). Theater screen: "Tartuffe."
France. End of the 18th century.
Paper, cardboard, wood, engraving, painting, printing, turned engraving.
43.5 x 24 cm.
Acquired in 1979 by I. V. and V. P. Cheremetiev.
10890/Pz-292

One side of the sheet represents a scene of a serenade in front of a house, in a framing of drawn flowers. On the other side the notes of an arietta are reproduced. One can also see a typographical inscription "A Paris chez Petit. Rue du Petit Pont à l'Image Notre Dame." It is believed that in the 18th century this fan was in the theater of the Palace of Ostankino.

Documentation: Catalogue of the exhibition of 1985, #16. Catalogue of the exhibition of 1987, #697.

26 (59). Theater screen: "The Barber of Seville."
France. End of the 18th century.
Paper, cardboard, wood, engraving, painting, printing, turned engraving.
43 x 24.5 cm.
10891/Pz-293

One side of the sheet represents a scene from the play, surrounded by drawings of flowers. The other side presents a part of the notes of the opera and the title is partly conserved: "The Barber of Seville, comedy. . ." Below is the typographical inscription "A Paris chez Petit. Rue du Petit Pont à l'Image Notre Dame." It is thought that in the 18th century this screen was in the theater of the Palace of Ostankino.

Documentation: Catalogue of the exhibition of 1980, #66. Catalogue of the exhibition of 1985, #17.

GERMANY

27 (60, 61). Two-sided fan: "The Wine Harvest." Frame with 21 mother-of-pearl blades.
Germany. Middle of the 18th century.
Paper, mother-of-pearl, paste, painting, sculpture, inlaying, gilding.
26.5 x 44.5 cm.
Among the acquisitions of 1968.
9415/Pz-252

In the centre of one side of the sheet a group is placed: two ladies and a knight are seated. The knight holds a vine branch in his hand. A little further away, a woman is stretched out carrying a basket on her head and we see a small boy sitting on a basket full of grapes. To the left, in the distance, a seated child is represented with a basket full of grapes and a woman who is dumping the grapes into a tub; to the right, a woman is spinning wool with the help of a distaff, to the side of her are a child and a sheep sleeping; on the other side, two women in a rural landscape are represented. The blades of the frame decorated in blue paste are indented with figures of a knight, two women, five cherubs and four Chinamen.

Documentation: Album "Ostankino." Catalogue of the exhibition of 1985, #18.

28 (62). Fan representing a pastoral scene. Frame with 18 shell blades.
Germany. Around 1760.
Paper, shell, painting, sculpture, gilding, silver, engraving, inlaying.
27.4 x 47.5 cm.
Gift of F. E. Vichnevski in 1958.

One side of the sheet represents, on the background of a rural landscape with a river, a couple of seated lovers. To their right, a villager tends a cow and a little boy plays with a goat. On the other side, a couple of musicians is presented on a background of a river and a bridge. On the blades of the frame are indented the figures of a trio of musicians and two cherubs. The panaches present some figures of men playing the violin.

Documentation: Catalogue of the

exhibition of 1956, #34. Album "Ostankino." Catalogue of the exhibition of 1985, #19.

29 (63). Two-sided fan representing a pastoral scene.

Frame with 19 bone blades.
Germany. Around 1760.
Paper, bone, painting, sculpture, engraving.
27 x 48 cm.
Gift of F. E. Vichnevski in 1958.
9241/Pz-214

One side of the sheet represents, in the centre, a mother with her two children and a dog walking on a path. Two travelers with sticks wander to meet them. In the far left, we see a house and two masculine figures. On the other side a landscape is drawn with ruins and the stamp of the customs port of St. Petersburg is affixed with the date: 1761. On the chiseled blades of the frame, a basket full of flowers is drawn with enamel colors. The panaches are decorated under the form of garlands of colored flowers and in relief.

Documentation: Catalogue of the exhibition of 1956, #35.

30 (70). Two-sided fan: "Couple of Lovers with the Cupids." Frame with 22 bone blades.
Germany. Around 1760.
Paper, bone, painting, sculpture, engraving, gilding.
29.5 x 51 cm.
Acquired in 1978 by I. I. Chmeleva
10818/Pz-283

In the centre of the completely painted sheet a young couple is represented: a knight plays the flute, a lady surrounded by two cupids holds flowers. To the right, a servant carries fruits. To the left, a kneeling woman picks flowers from bushes. On the other side a seated woman is represented on a landscape background. The blades are painted in gold and with diverse colors in the Chinese style: with some small figures, some fruit and some flowers. On the panaches are pierced grotesque half figures.

31 (64, 65). Two-sided fan: "Venus and Aurora." Frame with 20 mother-of-pearl blades.
Accompanied with a case covered in satin.
Germany. Around 1760.
Paper, mother-of-pearl, paste,

painting, sculpture, gilding.
27.5 x 59 cm.
Acquired in 1978 by S. M. Gorbatcheva. Previously this fan was part of the collection of L. I. Iakounina.
10892/Pz-294

One side of the sheet represents Venus and Aurora in a chariot. Two Cupids harness doves to the chariot. On the back, we can see a scene of a rendezvous in a park. The blades of the frame carry designs of birds, flowers, fruits and grass.

Documentation: Catalogue of the exhibition of 1980, #61.

32 (66, 67). Two-sided fan: "The Wash of Diana." Frame with 21 mother-of-pearl blades.
Germany. Around 1760.
Paper, mother-of-pearl, painting, sculpture, inlaying.
28.5 x 51 cm.
Acquired in 1985 by M. T. Androssov.
11470/Pz-365

One side of the sheet represents, on the background of a landscape, Diana seated among her servants. The other side represents a young girl with Cupid. In the central part of the blades are indented representations in relief of a young girl, a young man, and a flying Cupid.

33 (68, 69). Two-sided fan representing allegorical scenes. Frame with 22 mother-of-pearl and bone blades.
Germany. 1760's.
Paper, bone, mother-of-pearl, painting, sculpture.
27 x 42.5 cm.
Gift of F. E. Vichnevski in 1958.
9239/Pz-212

One side of the sheet represents, in the centre, a couple of lovers with Cupid. To the left, on a brown chariot, we see three cherubs, one of which is crowned with laurels. Behind them, in the distance, we can see a solitary boat with a passenger. To the right of the lovers is a Cupid-Cherub with a toy: a sheep on wheels, with which

a servant holding a basket of flowers plays. A small purse hangs from the servants belt. A little further to the right, a young couple walks, joined by a garland of flowers, and a seated lady plays the lyre. In the distance, Chronos watches from behind a rock as he contemplates all that is happening. The other side, the sheet represents a young couple seated in a park. The openwork bone blades, on which the figures of a lady at her table and four cherubs are represented, are placed on a mother-of-pearl base. On the mother-of-pearl panaches are indented figures of ladies.

34 (71). Fan: "The Rendezvous." Frame with 15 mother-of-pearl blades.
Germany. 1770-1780.
Paper, silk, mother-of-pearl, sequins, metallic thread, painting, sculpture, embroidery, engraving, gilding.
27 x 51.5 cm.
Gift of F. E. Vichnevski in 1958.
9242/Pz-215

In the centre of the silk sheet a scene of a declaration of love is represented which takes place under an arch near an altar. Cupid is holding a torch above the lovers. To the left a washstand with a parrot, a chair and a small bench are drawn, and to the right, a harp, a lute, a trunk and a stool. The blades represent ladies and cherubs.

Documentation: Catalogue of the exhibition of 1956, #56.

35 (73). Fan: "Gallant Scenes." Frame with 16 bone blades.
Germany. 1770-1780.
Silk, bone, sequins, metallic thread, painting, sculpture, embroidery, inlaying.
27.5 x 50 cm.
Gift of F. E. Vichnevski in 1958.
9244/Pz-217

In the centre of the silk sheet, surrounded by drawings of flowers, a knight holding a cane and a lady playing the lute are represented. On the other side the stamp of the customs port of St. Petersburg is

affixed.

Documentation: Catalogue of the exhibition of 1956, #38. Catalogue of the exhibition of 1985, #21.

36 (72). Fan: "The Rendezvous." Frame with 16 bone blades.
Germany. 1770-1780.
Silk, bone, gold and silver paper, metallic thread, sequins, painting, sculpture, engraving, inlaying, embroidery, appliqué.
28 x 52 cm.
Gift of F. E. Vichnevski in 1958.
9246/Pz-219

In the centre of the silk skeet a couple of lovers is represented seated in a park, with a child and a small dog to the side of them. The faces of the characters are original insertions in painted bone, which integrate harmoniously with the painting. On the panaches figures of ladies are indented. On the other side a customs stamp is found.

Documentation: Catalogue of the exhibition of 1956, #40. Catalogue of the exhibition of 1985, #22.

37 (76). Two-sided fan representing a gallant scene. Frame with 16 shell blades.
Germany. 1770-1780.
Paper, shell, silver and gold leaf, sequins, painting, sculpture, engraving, inlaying.
27.5 x 51 cm.
Gift of F. E. Vichnevski in 1958.
9248/Pz-231

The central cartel on one side of the sheet represents a seated knight holding a cage in his hand, on which a lady is leaning. A peasant carries flowers in a basket and a guard approaches them. On the other side motifs of flowers are drawn. The figures of a knight, some ladies and some ornamental compositions are inlaid on the blades in the metal leaf.

Documentation: Catalogue of the exhibition of 1956, #42.

38 (74, 75). Two-sided fan "The Rendezvous." Frame with 16 bone blades.
Germany. 1770-1780.
Paper, bone, sequins, painting, sculpture, embroidery, gilding.
26.5 x 48 cm.
Gift of F. E. Vichnevski in 1958.
9249/Pz-222

The central cartel on one side of the sheet represents a seated couple with a small dog. In the side cartels, we see a lady and a knight in some apartments. On the other side, a landscape is drawn in a frame of flower motifs. The panaches are indented with figures of cherubs.

Documentation: Catalogue of the exhibition of 1956, #43. Album "Ostankino." Catalogue of the exhibition of 1985, #23.

39 (77). Fan: "Family Scene." Frame with 16 pierced bone blades.

Germany. Around 1780.
Silk, bone, sequins, painting, sculpture, embroidery, inlaying.
28.5 x 54 cm.
Acquired in 1965 by I. I. Likhareva.
9308/Pz-232

The central cartel represents a family: to the right a woman holds a fan and is seated on a chair; in the centre, a man is standing with a riding crop in his hand; to the left, under a tree, a small boy holds a flying bird attached to a line, a hat is set at his feet. The side cartels present scenes of offerings of flowers. Between each large cartel, placed in a frame in the form of a vase, are two small cartels with birds and flowers. All the cartels are bordered with gold sequins. The pierced blades are inlaid with gold and silver leaf. On the other side of the sheet, on the right, the sales stamp is affixed: 1789. Chelko. tov. Moscow. This stamp covers another, on which we can make out : 1789. Boulek. T. V.

40 (79). Two-sided fan: "Couple of Musicians." Frame with 15 bone blades.
Germany. 1770-1780.
Bone, silk, sequins, paste, painting, sculpture, embroidery, inlaying.
25 x 48 cm.
Acquired in 1985 by N. V.

Ermolova.
11503/Pz-377

One side of the sheet represents, framed with motifs of flowers and decorations, a woman holding a partition of music, a man with a flute and a small boy. On the other side, we see a flowering branch.

41 (78). Two-sided fan representing parrots among flowers. Frame with 16 bone blades.
Germany. Around 1780.
Paper, silk, bone, paste, painting, sculpture, engraving, gilding.
28 x 46 cm.
Gift of F. E. Vichnevski in 1958.
9250/Pz-223

One side of the sheet represents two parrots sitting on some branches among flowers. To the side is an archway of twisting plants, a vase, some baskets of flowers and a watering can. On the other side a bouquet is drawn and the stamp of the customs of St.

Petersburg is affixed.

Documentation: Catalogue of the exhibition of 1956, #44.

42 (80, 81). Two-sided fan with three cartels. Frame with 17 mother-of-pearl blades.
Germany. Around 1780.
Paper, mother-of-pearl, silver leaf, painting, inlaying, gilding.
23.5 x 48 cm.
Acquired in 1979 by N. V. Chiriaeva.
10913/Pz-299

The central cartel, on one side of the sheet, represents a group composed of three ladies, a knight and a small boy carrying a cage with a bird. The left cartel shows a lady with a stick; the right, a seated knight with two dogs. On the other side a landscape with two figures is drawn. The panaches are indented with masculine figures.

Documentation: Catalogue of the exhibition of 1980, #62. Catalogue of the exhibition of 1985, #24.

43 (82). Fan representing a gallant scene. Frame with 14 bone blades.
Germany (?). Around 1780.
Silk, bone, paper, metal, glass, metallic thread and sequins, painting, sculpture, embroidery, engraving.
28 x 50 cm.
Acquired in 1982 by I. G. Smirnova.
11210/Pz-334

The centre of the sheet represents a seated couple, with a knight and a lady on the sides. The lady holds a fan in her hand.

Documentation: Catalogue of the exhibition of 1985, #25.

44 (83). Fan representing Cupid near an altar. Frame with 14 bone blades.
Germany. 1780-1790.
Silk, bone, sequins, sculpture, painting, engraving, embroidery, gilding.
28 x 50 cm.
Gift of F. E. Vichnevski in 1970.
9684/Pz-266

The silk sheet represents, in three

small cartels on a black background, among garlands and baskets of flowers, Cupid near an altar, in the central cartel, and two flaming hearts in the side cartels. On the panaches the figures of a young man holding some birds in his hands are indented.

45 (84). Two-sided fan: "Amusements in the Park." Frame with 14 bone blades.
Germany. End of the 1790's.
Paper, bone, painting, sculpture.
26.5 x 37 cm.
Acquired in 1984 by N. V. Ermolova.
11446/Pz-362

One side of the sheet represents a composition of five characters who are amusing themselves in a park. On the other side is a small sketch of a landscape and the inscription in ink: Von Französen. . .(unreadable) Grossmutter Schmidt. 1813 in Magdeburg. ("From the French. . . to Grandmother Schmidt. Madeburg 1813.")

46 (85). Fan representing an urban landscape with a river. Frame with 14 bone blades.
Germany. Around 1790.
Silk, bone silver leaf, sequins, painting, sculpture, embroidery, inlaying.
24.5 x 44.5 cm.
Gift of F. E. Vichnevski in 1958.
9251/Pz-224

On the silk sheet, in imitation engraving, a city is represented near a river, on which a small boat is sailing with a fisherman.

Documentation: Catalogue of the exhibition of 1956, #45. Catalogue of the exhibition of 1985, #26.

47 (86). Fan: "The Clemency of Alexander the Great." Frame with 14 bone blades.
Germany (Poland?). Middle of the 18th century.
Silk, skins, bone, leather, painting, sculpture, engraving.
29 x 52.5 cm.
Acquired in 1965 by E. P. Olkina.
9307/Pz-231

The skin sheet represents

Alexander the Great before his tent facing a group of kneeling prisoners. To the left, further away, we see three masculine figures. One of them is dressed as a lansquenet, the second, as a Turk, and the third in a Polish or Hungarian (?) costume. To the right a chariot with trophies is found, among which we see a cage with a parrot. The manner of the painting on the skin recalls points of embroidery. The panaches are covered with bands of leather

carrying an ornamental engraving.

Documentation: Catalogue of the exhibition of 1985, #27.

ENGLAND

48 (19, 88). Fan with three cartels: "Rural Scene." Frame with 16 bone blades.
England. Around 1790.
Silk, paper, bone, sequins, paste, painting, silk engraving, sculpture, embroidery.
28.5 x 52 cm.
Gift of F. E. Vichnevski in 1958.
9229/Pz-202

Among the drawings of flowers situated in the round cartels framed with sequins three silk engravings are represented. The central cartel represents a scene of rural life: a lady standing while leaning against a branch, a servant carrying a bucket, and some children playing on the side. In the side cartels, we see two bacchantes and Cupid. On the other side the stamp of the customs port of Ravel is affixed and the date: 1791.

Documentation: Catalogue of the exhibition of 1956, #23. Album "Ostankino." Catalogue of the exhibition of 1985, #33.

49 (89). Fan representing an allegorical scene: "The Young Girls

and Love." Frame with 20 bone blades.
England. Around 1790.
Silk, bone, sequins, silver paper, painting, sculpture, engraving, inlaying.
24.5 x 45 cm.
Gift of F. E. Vichnevski in 1958.
9231/Pz-204

On the background of a landscape four young girls are represented, two of which hold a small Cupid by the hand. In the sky two doves fly.

Documentation: Catalogue of the exhibition of 1956, #25. Catalogue of the exhibition of 1985, #29.

50 (90). Fan: "The Coronation." Frame with 19 bone blades.
England. Second half of the 1790's.
Silk, bone, sequins, lace, painting, sculpture, embroidery.
24 x 44 cm.
Gift of F. E. Vichnevski in 1958.
9230/Pz-203

On a background of greenery, a couple of lovers are seated, a knight places a crown of flowers on the lady's head. On the blades are representations of a knight, a lady and architectural motifs are indented.

Documentation: Catalogue of the exhibition of 1956, #24. Catalogue of the exhibition of 1985, #28.

51 (87). Fan: "Dance with a Drum." Frame with 18 bone blades.
England. Second half of the 1790's.
Silk, bone, sequins, silk engraving, sculpture, embroidery, gilding.
23 x 41 cm.
Gift of F. E. Vichnevski in 1958.
9232/Pz-205

The silk sheet represents, in an oval, due to the technique of painted engraving, an antique dancer with a Basque drum. The oval is framed with sequins and on each side, with the help of sequins, bands of poppies with ripe capsules are embroidered. The sheet is surmounted with a festoon ornament embroidered with gold

sequins.

Documentation: Catalogue of the exhibition of 1956, #26.

52 (91). Fan with three cartels: "Werther." Frame with 15 bone blades.
England. Around 1790.
Silk, bone, paper, sequins, engraving, sculpture, embroidery, gilding.
28 x 52.5 cm.
Gift of F. E. Vichnevski in 1958.
9227/Pz-200

Engravings are glued on the sheet and framed with sequins. In the centre, one sees a scene inspired by the novel by J. W. Goethe, "The Sufferings of Young Werther." A young man is seated at a table and he is writing a letter. To the side of him is a young woman in an attitude of despair and a small boy carrying a pistol. The side cartels show painted representations on the theme of antique reliefs. On the other side the stamp of the customs port of St. Petersburg is affixed with the date: 1791.

Documentation: Catalogue of the exhibition of 1956, #21.

53 (92). Fan: "Children's Games." Frame with 16 bone blades.
England. Around 1790.
Silk, paper, bone, paste, sequins, painting, engraving, sculpture.
28 x 53 cm.
Gift of F. E. Vichnevski in 1958.
9228/Pz-201

Three ovals in paper are glued on the sheet of silk, framed with sequins. In the one in the centre, a technique of engraving reproduces a child's game. A small girl holds a whip and is seated in a wagon pulled by two small boys and pushed by a third. The ovals on the side consist of symbolic representations: to the left, a torch and some kissing doves; and to the

right, a quiver of arrows.

54 (94). Fan with ornamental motifs. Frame with 18 bone blades.
England. Around 1790.
Silk, bone, sequins, silk thread, paste, metal leaf, embroidery, sculpture, gilding, inlaying.
24.5 x 45 cm.
Gift of F. E. Vichnevski in 1958.
9233/Pz-206

On the silk sheet, sequins form an embroidery of flowers and geometric figures. The panaches are abundantly set with paste (the small pieces of glass imitate precious stones).

Documentation: Catalogue of the exhibition of 1956, #27. Album "Ostankino." Catalogue of the exhibition of 1985, #30.

55 (95). Fan representing a bouquet of sequins. Frame with 19 horn blades, inlaid with steel sequins.
England. Second half of the 1790's.
Satin, horn, sequins, silk thread, embroidery, inlaying.
24 x 44.5 cm.
Gift of F. E. Vichnevski in 1958.
9234/Pz-207

The silk sheet is embroidered with a large bouquet in sequins and in multicolored thread.

Documentation: Catalogue of the exhibition of 1956, #28. Catalogue of the exhibition of 1985, #32.

56 (28, 93). Fan with ornamental motifs. Frame with 17 bone blades.
England. End of the 18th century.
Silk, bone, sequins, silk thread, sculpture, embroidery, gilding.
18.5 x 36.6 cm.
Gift of F. E. Vichnevski in 1958.
9235/Pz-208

The silk sheet carries ornamental sequin ovals serving as strips polished like mirrors.

Documentation: Catalogue of the exhibition of 1956, #29. Album "Ostankino." Catalogue of the exhibition of 1985, #31.

ITALY

57 (97, 98). Two-sided fan: "Dawn." Frame with 20 shell blades.
Italy. 1760-1770.
Skin, mother-of-pearl, shell, bone, bronze, painting, sculpture, inlaying, gilding.
28.5 x 51 cm.
Acquired in 1975.
1004/Pz-270

One side of the skin sheet represents a famous fresco by Guido Reni, taken from the palazzo of Cardinal Scipion Borghese (today the Palazzo Pallavincini Rospigliosi). But the composition is presented "as a reflection in a mirror" (reversed from right to left). Ordered by Aurora, surrounded by female figures, symbolizing a clock, a solar chariot in which is found Apollo moving through the sky. On the other side a marine port with a lighthouse, a fortress and a boat is drawn. The panaches are inlaid in gilded bronze with figures of Cupids and bacchantes at the foot of a vine.

Documentation: Catalogue of the exhibition of 1985, #11.

58 (96). Fan with three cartels: "The Pantheon." Frame with 16 bone blades.
Italy. Around 1780.
Parchment, wood, bone, painting, sculpture, inlaying.
28.5 x 48 cm.
Gift of F. E. Vichnevski in 1958.
9252/Pz-225

On the parchment sheet, three cartels represent antique edifices. The central cartel shows the Pantheon of Rome; the right, the ruins of a stone arch; the left, a funeral monument.

Documentation: Catalogue of the exhibition of 1956, #46. Album "Ostankino." Catalogue of the exhibition of 1985, #34.

59 (99). Painted fan sheet in the style of Pompeii presented in three cartels.
Italy. Around 1780.
Paper, painting.

15 x 43.5 cm.
Gift of F. E. Vichnevski in 1958.
9457/Pz-255

The central cartel represents antique characters: a couple of lovers drawing; the side cartels represent some antique ruins. The cartels are framed with motifs inspired by frescoes of Pompeii.

Documentation: Catalogue of the exhibition of 1985, #35.

60 (100). Fan sheet representing a landscape with a waterfall.
Italy. 1780-1790.
Paper, cardboard, painting.
15 x 43.5 cm.
Acquired in 1968 by M. I. Kalinina.
9457/Pz-256

In the central cartel a landscape with a large waterfall and two figures in the foreground is represented. In the cartels to the left and right, are motifs of the ancient world.

Documentation: Catalogue of the exhibition of 1985, #36.

61 (101). Fan with three cartels in the style of the frescoes of Pompeii. Frame with 20 shell blades.
Italy. End of the 18th century.
Paper, shell, metal leaf, painting, sculpture, engraving, inlaying, gilding.
23.5 x 48 cm.
Gift of F. E. Vichnevski in 1958.
9253/Pz-226

The central cartel represents Cupid in an arch, treading on an open book. In the side cartels, we see a pigeon with a flower.

Documentation: Catalogue of the exhibition of 1956, #47. Album "Ostankino." Catalogue of the exhibition of 1985, #37.

62 (102). Fan sheet: "The Ruins of the Antique Temple."
Italy. End of the 18th century.
Painting on skin.
17.5 x 35.5 cm.
Acquired in 1986 by L. G. Goubarvea.
11561/Pz-398

63 (103). Fan sheet: "The Ruins of

the Antique Circus."
Italy. End of the 18th century.
Painting on skin.
17.5 x 35.5 cm.
Acquired in 1986 by L. G. Goubareva.
11562/Pz-399

HOLLAND

64 (104). Screen in mica representing figures of women.
Holland (Colony of Indochina?).
End of the 17th – beginning of the 18th century.
Wood, mica, paper-maché, cardboard, leather, silk, painting, sculpture, gilding.
36.6 x 33 cm.
Acquired in 1968 by M. I. Kalinina.
9456/Pz-254

On the sheet of transparent mica, surrounded by a fringe of multicolored silk, two figures of half-naked women and motifs of vegetation are drawn. The carved handle is covered with colored leather, painted in places with gold.

Documentation: Album "Ostankino." Catalogue of the exhibition of 1985, #38.

65 (107, 109). Two-sided fan painted in the "chinoiserie" style. Frame with 14 mixed blades.
Holland. Around 1780.
Paper, bone, wood, shell, mother-of-pearl, mica, lacquer, metal leaf, fabric, painting, sculpture, inlaying, appliqué.
29.5 x 53.5 cm.
Acquired in 1968 by M. I. Kalinina.
9455/Pz-253

On the paper sheet is the following image, at the same time painted and applied: a large bouquet, on the background of which two landscapes with pagodas placed in frames are presented. To the left and to the right are small scenes of Chinese genre in interiors. The blades are constituted of mother-of-pearl, shell and bone. On the other side objects of daily Chinese life are drawn.

19TH CENTURY

RUSSIA

66 (114). Fan with 22 horn blades, executed in gothic style and decorated with sequins.
Russia. 1820-1830.
Horn, metallic sequins, silk, sculpture, inlaying, bone painting.
19 x 36 cm.
Arrived in 1981 from the Museum of Porcelain in the Château "Kouskovo" of the 18th Century. Coming from the private collection of the famous Muscovite L. I. Rouzskaïa.
11009/Pz-318

Documentation: Catalogue of the exhibition of 1985, #40.

67 (117). Fan with five painted cartels and 15 painted bone blades.
Russia. St. Petersburg (?). Around 1830.
Silk, bone, gold sequins, openwork blades in steel, painting, sculpture, embroidery.
21.7 x 41 cm.
Acquired in 1982 by G. N. Vsesviatskaïa.
11247/Pz-337

The central cartel of the silk sheet represents a couple of lovers on a background of a landscape with a church. In the side cartels seated figures are placed: on the left, a woman; on the right, a man. The half cartels, at the extremities, present flowers. Along with sequins, the sheet is decorated with openwork and fashioned blades in oxidized steel. On the panaches a trio of musicians is painted.

Documentation: Catalogue of the exhibition of 1985, #39.

68 (122, 123). Two-sided fan with a painting in ink. Frame with 16 wood blades.
Russia. 1850-1860.
Wood, leather, mother-of-pearl, silk, sculpture, weaving, ink painting.
24 x 42.5 cm.
Acquired in 1986 by N. V. Diligenskaïa.

11566/Pz-403

Drawn on one of the sides of the thick wood blades are: in the centre, the letter S carrying above it a princely crown; at the upper ends of the blades, we see the contour of a man and woman's head, portraits in their genre, and below them, some inscriptions in French, the contents of which vary (memories, puns, praises to the owner of the fan, etc.). On the other side of the sheet, in the centre, grotesque human figures placed horizontally, form the name: Séraphine. On the upper part of the blades heads resembling portraits are also drawn, with inscriptions (autographs) below them and a French maxim. The autographs belong to Nekhlioudov, Le Delobel, Basilévitch, Jazikovaïa, the Baron Guerik and others. The panaches are covered with black leather. According to the owner, the fan belonged to his great grand-mother Séraphine Vladimirovna Volkonskaïa.

69 (125). Fan with a silk sheet, set with sequins. Frame with 18 bone blades.
Russia. Around 1870.
Silk, bone, mother-of-pearl, metallic sequins, sculpture, embroidery, weaving, braiding.
27 x 51 cm.
Acquired in 1967 by M. A. Tchoudakova.
9378/Pz-239

Documentation: Catalogue of the exhibition of 1985, #46.

70 (127). Fan with a silk sheet, painted with small flowers. Frame with 16 mother-of-pearl blades. With case covered with satin.
Russia. Around 1870.
Silk, satin, cardboard, embroidered paper, typographical printing, embroidery, sculpture.
26.8 x 51 cm.
Acquired in 1984 in an antique shop, at Moskomissiontorg #15.
11375/Pz-358

In the interior of the case the original label is glued: "Moret Store on the Kouznetski bridge,

Solodovnikova house in Moscow. Gifts. H. Moret. Moscow." The embroidery of the sheet has disappeared.

71 (128). Lace fan decorated with a painting. Frame with 18 bone blades.
Russia. Around 1870.
Bone, silk, lace, painting, sculpture, weaving.
32 x 52 cm.
Acquired in 1984 by N. V. Ermolova.
11447/Pz-363

The sheet of silk lace is painted with flowers, a young girl holding a lyre, and Cupid.

72 (130). Lace fan representing frolicking Cupids. Frame with 18 bone blades.
Russia. Around 1880.
Lace, silk, bone, painting, sculpture, engraving, weaving.
35 x 71 cm.
Acquired in 1975 by S. N. Alferieva.
10085/Pz-275

Documentation: Catalogue of the exhibition of 1985, #42.

73 (131). Fan of white ostrich feathers. Frame with 17 mother-of-pearl blades.
Russia. Around 1880.
Mother-of-pearl, ostrich feathers, sculpture.
48 x 77.5 cm.
Acquired in 1978 by E. B. Tchijova.
10845/Pz-285

Documentation: Catalogue of the exhibition of 1985, #44.

74 (129). Silk fan with painted lace representing flowers and bees. Frame with 18 bone blades.
Russia. Around 1880.
Silk, lace, bone, painting, weaving.
35 x 66.5 cm.
Acquired in 1981 in an antique shop at Moskomissiontorg #15.
11027/Pz-320

Documentation: Catalogue of the exhibition of 1985, #74.

75 (132). Satin fan representing a bouquet. Frame with 18 bone blades.
Russia. Around 1880.

Satin, bone, wood, metal, silk thread, painting, sculpture, milling, twisting.
35 x 66.5 cm.
Acquired in 1980 by N. G. Maximova.
10983/Pz-310

Documentation: Catalogue of the exhibition of 1985, #73.

76 (133). Fan with a sheet of silk gauze and lace painted with bouquets of edelweiss and flowering branches. Frame with 18 pierced bone blades.
Russia. Around 1880.
Silk, lace, bone, metal, painting, sculpture, weaving, braiding.
36 x 67 cm.
Acquired in 1984 by T. G. Syrkina.
11391/Pz-350

77 (134). Satin fan painted with flowers and carrying the inscription: "souvenir." Frame with 18 bone blades.
Russia. 1880-1890.
Satin, bone, metal, painting, sculpture.
32 x 61 cm.
Acquired in 1979 by E. M. Koudrina-Borissoglebskaïa.
10918/Pz-304

Documentation: Catalogue of the exhibition of 1985, #50.

78 (135). Fan with a blue silk sheet, decorated with an appliqué of embroidered lace. Frame with 16 pierced bone blades.
Russia. Around 1890.
Bone, silk, lace, mother-of-pearl, metal, sculpture, weaving, appliqué.
21.7 x 49 cm.
Acquired in 1986 by V. I. Zamertseva.
11563/Pz-400

79 (139). Flowered lace fan, the silk sheet of which is decorated with sequins. Frame with 16 bone blades.
Alexandre House.
Accompanied by a case in cardboard. Bone, silk, sequins, metallic thread, painting, sculpture, weaving, braiding, engraving.
21.5 x 40.5 cm.

Acquired in 1982 in an antique shop at Moskomissiontorg #15.
11199/Pz-332

The label in the interior of the case carries the inscription: "Alexandre, maker of umbrellas, fans, lathe works and works in leather. St. Petersburg, Perspective Nevski, #11." The frame was created in France and the sheet decorated in Russia. The whole of the fan was put together in the workshop of the Alexandre House in St. Petersburg.

Documentation: Catalogue of the exhibition of 1985, #43.

80 (136). Fan with 20 openwork bone blades.
Russia. End of the 19th century.
Bone, silk, mother-of-pearl, sculpture, weaving.
27 x 35 cm.
Acquired in 1967 by M. A. Tchoudakova.
9379/Pz-240

Documentation: Catalogue of the exhibition of 1985, #47.

81 (140). Fan in black ostrich feathers. Frame with 17 shell blades.
Russia. End of the 19th century.
Shell, ostrich feathers, sculpture.
34 x 66 cm.
Acquired in 1968 by A. G. Gladkovskaïa.
9657/Pz-263

Documentation: Catalogue of the exhibition of 1985, #48.

82 (141). Lace fan. Frame with 18 bone blades.
Russia. End of the 19th century.
Lace, bone, mother-of-pearl, metal, sculpture, engraving.
24.5 x 46 cm.
Gift of M. K. and K. K. Gladkovski in 1973.
10002/Pz-268

Documentation: Catalogue of the exhibition of 1985, #49.

83 (142). Lace fan. Frame with 18 mother-of-pearl blades.
Accompanied by a case in cardboard.
Russia. End of the 19th century.
Lace, silk, bone, mother-of-pearl,

metal, sculpture, painting, fleecing.
21.1 x 50 cm.
Acquired in 1983 by L. N. Vigdorovitch.
11281/Pz-340

Documentation: Catalogue of the exhibition of 1985, #51.

84 (145). Fan fashioned in pheasant feathers. Frame with 16 shell blades.
Russia. End of the 19th century.
Shell, feathers, sculpture, arrangement.
24 x 37 cm.
Acquired in 1985 by L. G. Savtchenko.
11518/Pz-418

85 (144). Fan with a sheet of silk and lace. Frame with 18 mother-of-pearl blades. Accompanied by a case.
Russia. End of the 19th century.
Silk, mother-of-pearl, lace, sequins, sculpture, painting, embroidery, braiding, weaving.
29.5 x 54.5 cm.
Acquired in 1986 by N. A. Pletneva.
11673/Pz-432

On the silk sheet garlands of flowers interlaced with a ribbon are placed.

86 (146). Fan with a sheet of black watered fabric. Frame with 14 wood blades, openwork and pierced.
Russia. End of the 19th century.
Wood, metal, sculpture, weaving.
27.5 x 52 cm.
Acquired in 1986 by N. P. Pigareva.
1168/Pz-435

This fan belonged to the grand-daughter of the poet F. I. Tioutchev, E. I. Pigareva (née Tioutchev).

87 (147). Lace fan carrying the monogram A. A. Tatischeva. Frame with 18 cellulose blades.
Accompanied by a cardboard case.
Russia. End of the 19th century.
Lace, cellulose, metal, weaving, sculpture, gilding.
27 x 53 cm.
Acquired in 1981 by A. V. Kamenskaïa.
11150/Pz-327

One of the panaches carries the monogram in gilded bronze: A. T. This fan belonged to the countess Tatischeva Alexandra Alexandrovna (née Volodimerova), wife of the member of the Ministry of the Interior, the count V. S. Tatischev (Tatischev S. S., The Tatischevs. 1400-1900. Historical and Genealogical Study. St. Petersburg, 1900, p. 165).

Documentation: Catalogue of the exhibition of 1985, #45.

88 (148). Fan representing a bouquet of flowers. Frame with 16 bone blades.
Russia. End of the 19th century – beginning of the 20th century.
Silk, bone, grains of glass, sequins, metal leaf, painting, sculpture, embroidery, engraving, weaving, inlaying.
20.5 x 65 cm.
Acquired in 1968 by A. G. Gladkovskaïa.
9658/Pz-264

The sheet, in transparent silk represents, a bouquet composed of a green branch, roses and blue flowers. Along the panaches, the sheet has steel sequins with little grains of transparent glass on the interior.

89 (149). Fan with a sheet of blue feathers. Frame with 11 blue wood blades.
Russia. End of the 19th century – beginning of the 20th century.
Wood, feathers, sculpture, engraving, painting in silver and blue gouache.
22.5 x 49 cm.
Acquired in 1979 by G. M. Koudrina-Borissoglebskaïa.
10917/Pz-303

90 (150). Fan with a sheet of white ostrich feathers. Frame with 20 cellulose blades.
Russia. End of the 19th century – beginning of the 20th century.
Feathers, cellulose, silk, metal, sculpture, melting, weaving.
32 x 54 cm.
Acquired in 1985 by G. I. Baumstein.
11505/Pz-379

91 (152). Fan in the form of a screen. Frame with 20 pierced bladed in gutta-percha carrying motifs of flowers.
Russia. End of the 19th century – beginning of the 20th century.
Silk, gutta-percha, weaving, sculpture.
22.7 x 15 cm.
Acquired in 1985 by V. N. Naourits.
11507/Pz-381

92 (153). Fan with a painted sheet. Frame with 16 bone blades.
Russia. End of the 19th century – beginning of the 20th century.
Silk, bone, sculpture, weaving.
32.5 x 61.5 cm.
Acquired in 1986 by M. V. Milman.
11625/Pz-413

The silk sheet represents a rose branch, forget-me-nots, and white flowers.

UKRAINE

93 (151). Two-sided fan: "The Rural Marriage." Frame with 15 shell blades.
Painted by B. Slavzinski.
Ukraine. Around 1860.
Shell, skin, painting, sculpture.
30 x 50 cm.
Acquired in 1981 by E. I. Gorelik.
11151/Pz-328

One side of the skin sheet represents a marriage ceremony in the street of a rural Ukrainian village. To the right, at the bottom, is found the inscription: B. Slavzinski. The other side carries family coats of arms: on a blue background a shield is represented with a crescent of the moon, the tips of which point to the sky, with a golden star above it. The shield carries the crown of a count crowned with five ostrich feathers. The coat of arms is called "Leliwa." It has been famous since the 12th century and belonged to numerous (more than 120) Polish families residing in Poland as well as in other countries (Juliusz hr. Ostrowski. Ksiega hervowa rodow polskich. Warszawa, 1897. Str. 39-43; 177-178, tabl 1739-1751). The owner of this fan came from the family of the count Tarnovski,

whose lands were found in the provinces of Volynie and of Podolie. (Leszczyc Zbigniew. Herby szlachty polskiej. Lwow, 1908, T. I. Leliwa).

Documentation: Catalogue of the exhibition of 1985, #41.

FRANCE

94 (155). Fan: "Family Scene." Frame with 16 bone blades.
France. Beginning of the 19th century.
Paper, bone, painted engraving, sculpture.
18.8 x 26 cm.
Acquired in 1985 by K. V. Kouvydrine.
11440/Pz-417

The paper sheet represents a family scene. To the right, a lady is seated in a chair of the Empire style, with armrests in the form of griffons. To the left, leaning on a rifle, a man is standing with dogs at his feet. In the centre a small boy and a small girl dancing while holding hands are represented. All the characters are dressed in the costume of the 19th century.

Documentation: Catalogue of the exhibition of 1985, #79.

95 (162, 163). Two-sided fan: "The Reception at the Lord's House." Frame with 18 pierced bone blades.
France. Around 1840.
Paper, bone, down, lithograph, painting, sculpture.
26.5 x 48 cm.
Acquired in 1987 by A. A. Grodski.
11697/Pz-440

The paper sheet represents, on one side, in a framing of decorative motifs, a lithograph, in color, of a scene of a reception of guests at the house of a lord. In the centre, on a background of a castle and park, the couple of owners are seated at a table and welcome the guests standing to the right, with two small babies. An embarrassed young woman is also standing, a fan in her hand. To the left, are all the inhabitants of the house. The representation is inspired by a literary subject. On the other side

a landscape is drawn with a house and a river and on each side are vignettes in silver.

96 (164, 165). Two-sided fan: "The Young Sirens." Frame with 16 mother-of-pearl blades.
France. Middle of the 19th century.
Paper, mother-of-pearl, gold leaf, painting, sculpture, inlaying, gilding.
27.5 x 52 cm.
Gift of F. E. Vichnevski in 1958.
9223/Pz-196

In the centre, on one side of the sheet, five young girls in antique costume are represented on the bank of a river, in the shade of trees. In the side medallions, to the left and right, couples of lovers are drawn. On the other side, we see a pastoral scene: two male and two female shepherds, to the side of which is a sleeping dog. A little further away are sheep. On the blades, inlaid with gold leaf, are representations of two ladies, a knight and motifs of vegetation.

Documentation: Catalogue of the exhibition of 1956, #17.

97 (166). Fan: "Gallant Scene." Frame with 18 mother-of-pearl blades.
France. Middle of the 19th century.
Paper, mother-of-pearl, gold and silver leaf, bronze, painting, sculpture, inlaying.
27 x 51 cm.
Gift of F. E. Vichnevski in 1958.
9225/Pz-198

One side of the sheet represents a gallant group in a park. To the left, a lady is seated in a chair with a fan in her hand. Facing her is a seated young girl holding a book. Two young ladies and two knights are standing next to them. A young woman approaches them from the right. On the other side a landscape with a bridge is drawn.

Documentation: Catalogue of the exhibition of 1956, #19.

98 (168). Two-sided fan: "The Reception with the King." Frame with 14 bone blades.
France. Middle of the 19th century.
Paper, bone, painting, lithograph in

color, sculpture, gilding.
27 x 50.5 cm.
Gift of F. E. Vichnevski in 1958.
9226/Pz-199

One side of the sheet represents, in the centre, a child-king seated on a throne, surrounded by courtesans. On the other side, we see a scene taken from an oriental legend. In the centre, a beautiful woman is lying on a couch and surrounded by eleven young girls. A winged genie covers the woman with flowers. At her feet, a man in a turban kneels. The arabesques which carry the blades and the panaches are covered with painting in gold and silver.

Documentation: Catalogue of the exhibition of 1956, #20.

99 (169, 170). Two-sided fan.
Frame with 16 bone blades.
France. Around 1850.
Paper, bone, silver and gold leaf, painting, sculpture, inlaying.
22.5 x 50.5 cm.
Acquired in 1967 by L. N. Rapporport.
9654/Pz-260

One side of the sheet represents an august family: a couple and four children. To the left of the central group a knight and a seated lady are found, a fan in her hand; to the right, we see two young girls washing their feet in a stream. The other side represents a group composed of two women and five children and a dog standing on the seashore.

Documentation: Catalogue of the exhibition of 1985, #57.

100 (167). Two-sided fan representing a scene of rural life.
Frame with 18 mother-of-pearl blades.
France. Middle of the 19th century.
Silk, mother-of-pearl, paste, bronze, down, painting, sculpture, melting.
26.5 x 51 cm.
Arrived in 1981 from the Museum of Porcelain in the Kouskovo Château of the 18th century.
Coming from the collection of L. I. Rouszkaïa.

110008/Pz-317

The one side of the sheet represents a group composed of eight peasants. On the other side color vignette is found. The sheet is covered with white down. A tassel with gold cords is pinned to the fan.

101 (172, 173). Two-sided fan.
Frame with 20 mother-of-pearl blades.
The author of the painting is Gérinçau.
Accompanied by a case covered with blue velour and white satin.
France. 1850-1860.
Paper, mother-of-pearl, metal, painting, sculpture, engraving.
28 x 53 cm.
Acquired in 1967 by I. N. Rapporport.
9653/Pz-259

One side of the sheet represents a group of young people in a forest. In the centre is a seated young man. He holds in his hand a cage with a bird. To the side of him are three young girls. To the left, next to them, are three sheep. To the right, a young couple with flowers.

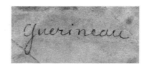

In the distance, behind some bushes, we see a second couple. To the left on the sheet is the signature: Gérinçau. On the other side, in the large central cartel, are a seated young girl and two small boys with small sheep. In the left cartel, we see two cherubs playing music and in the right cartel two cherubs reading a book. The panaches were later restored and fixed with appliqués of brass which carry the engraved inscription: To the lovely Militchka from Tcherepakhov 24/IX-39. In the interior of the case, engraved in gold is Alexandre: fan maker to their majesties: The Empress of France, the Empress of Russia, the Queen of England, the Queen of Spain, 14, Boulevard Montmartre, Paris.

102 (174, 175). Two-sided fan representing a group of musicians.
Frame with 18 chiseled mother-of-pearl blades. Accompanied by a cardboard case covered with satin.
France. 1850-1860.
Paper, mother-of-pearl, colored lithograph, painting, sculpture.
27 x 51 cm.
Acquired in 1985 in the antique shop at Moskomissiontorg #15.
11545/Pz-388

One side of the sheet represents a group of musicians composed of five people. On the other side, we see a group of five peasants near a river.

103 (176, 177). Two-sided fan: "The Victory of Amphitrite."
Frame with 13 chiseled, gilded mother-of-pearl blades.
Accompanied by a case covered with velvet.
France. Around 1860.
Paper, mother-of-pearl, sculpture, lithograph, typographical printing, glass, opal, gilding.
28 x 53 cm.
Acquired in 1984 in the antique shop at Moskomissiontorg #15.
11407/Pz-355

One side of the sheet represents, in three cartels, lithographic images. The central cartel presents Amphitrite, sailing in a boat pulled by swans and framed with Cupids, elves, sirens, and nymphs. The right cartel shows Cupid, some elves and kissing doves. The left cartel depicts three Graces and some elves. On the other side, in five cartels are: in the two main cartels, a male and female shepherd, and in the others, bouquets of flowers in vases. On the panaches figures in the costume of the 17th century are indented: to one side, a woman; the other, a falconer with a bird in his hand. In the interior of the case is glued the ticket: Antique fans. Fans for baskets. House Ernest Kees. Specialized in repair. 9 Boulevard des Capucines, Paris. Fans, jeweler, jewelry and lace. (The famous French company Ernest Kees, created in the 1860's, existed until the beginning of the

20th century. Many famous painters and fan specialists worked there (cf.: The Fan. Mirror of the Belle Époque, p. 146).

104 (178, 179). Marriage fan painted on both sides. Frame with 20 openwork mother-of-pearl blades. Painted by Calamatta. From motifs of the painter Picou. Accompanied by a case in cardboard covered in satin. France. Around 1870. Paper, silk, mother-of-pearl, sculpture, painting, gilding, weaving, inlaying with gold and

silver leaf, braiding. 28 x 60 cm. Arrived in 1981 from the Museum of Porcelain in the Kouskovo Château of the 18th century. Coming from the collection of L. I. Rouszkaïa. 11004/Pz-313

One side of the sheet represents a scene of the dressing of a bride before the ceremony. On the other side, we see a chair with some small Cupids on each side, a knight and a young girl. In the side medallions Cupids praising the bride are drawn. To the right is the signature: Calamatta according to Picou. On the back of the right panache, one can read the inscription in ink: Alexandre. In the interior of the lid of the case Mag. H. Moret is inscribed in gold. According to the inscriptions,

this fan was created by the Alexandre house and was sold in the store of Moret in Moscow. Josephine Calamatta (née Rochette) was born in Paris and

died in 1893. Married to the famous painter and lithographer Luigi Calamatta (1802-1869), she was a portrait and genre painter. In 1875, in the sale exhibition of the Alexandre house, one of her fans was sold which carried the inscription "The Triumph of Venus" (cf.: Benezit, Vol. 2, p. 451). Henri Pierre Picou (1824-1895), genre painter (cf.: Benezit, Vol. 8, p. 310). The two painters were specialists in the painting of fans.

Documentation: Catalogue of the exhibition of 1985, #52.

105 (180). Fan: "The Rendezvous." Frame with 18 mother-of-pearl blades. Painted by Imvert. Accompanied by a cardboard case. France. 1870-1880. Silk, lace, mother-of-pearl, painting, sculpture, weaving. 25 x 68 cm. Acquired in 1985 by E. M. Savonina. 11471/Pz-366

The silk sheet represents, in a framing of lace, the meeting of a young couple: a knight holding bouquets of flowers and a lady with a fan. Under the drawing is the signature: Imbert. The bottom of the case carries the inscription in ink: Weiss Berlin, Gasse m/Spitze. L. R. Jean-François Imbert. Died in 1887. Painter of portraits and designer (cf.: Benezit, Vol. 5, p. 710).

106 (181). Fan in black tulle. Frame with 18 shell blades. Accompanied by a cardboard case. France. Around 1880. Shell, tulle, lace, metallic sequins, sculpture, weaving, embroidery, appliqué. 32.5 x 61.5 cm. Acquired in 1969 by V. N. Troukhanov. 9460/Pz-257

The dark shell blades, abundantly inlaid with metallic sequins, are fixed to a sheet of black tulle, on which is applied a composition in white lace representing lilac branches and garlands of flowers.

The entire background is abundantly covered in metallic sequins, which give the fan a somber and mysterious beauty. In the interior of the case is the inscription in stamped gold: Ernest Kees. Maker of fans. 9 Boulevard des Capucines. Paris.

107 (182). Fan: "The Flight of Juno." Frame with 15 chiseled

mother-of-pearl blades. Painted by Marie Dumas inspired by a watercolor by Louis Leloir. France. Around 1880. Paper, mother-of-pearl, sculpture, engraving, gilding. 35.5 x 67.5 cm. Acquired in 1965 by N. V. Palmstveig. 9372/Pz-233

The paper sheet represents Juno flying in a chariot driven by swallows. She is accompanied by Aurora and Flora, who toss flowers from a basket carried by Cupid. The chiseled blades carry the representation in gold of a gallant couple in the costume of the 18th century. On the panaches cherub-knights and crossed torches are indented. To the left, the sheet carries the signature : M. Dumas. The composition of the painting is created after a watercolor by the painter Louis Leloir (cf.: Blondel S. Intimate Art and Taste in France.

Paris, 1884, p. 74, fig. 33). Marie Dumas was a miniaturist painter, specialized in the painting of fans. (cf.: The Great French Encyclopedia. Vol. 16, p. 884). In the 1890's she worked in the Kees house (The Fan, Mirror of the Belle Époque, p. 148). Alexandre-

Louis Leloir (1843-1884) was a painter, watercolorist and engraver. He was the founder of the French Society of Watercolorists and the author of numerous watercolors. He was very famous as a fan painter of subjects in the style of the 18th century. (cf.: Benezit, Vol. 6, p. 558).

Documentation: Catalogue of the exhibition of 1985, #55.

108 (185). Fan sheet: "Poucelina." France. Around 1880. Painted by Marie Dumas. Silk, lace, painting, weaving. 18 x 63 cm. Acquired by V. N. Peterson in 1981. 11149/Pz-326

In the lace sheet representing tulips and other flowers, on the left side, a piece of painted silk is inserted: a young girl holding a fan in her right hand and lying against a branch of a flowering tree. Under the drawing is found the signature: M. Dumas. The sheet is detached from a frame of 18 pierced mother-of-pearl blades elegantly engraved, unfortunately very damaged and conserved separately in a case covered with satin and lined with silk. The interior of the cover of the case carries the inscription in gold: 17 passage Panoramas. Duvelleroy. 35, Blvd des Capucines.

109 (183). Fan with a lace sheet. Frame with 17 gilded mother-of-pearl blades. Accompanied by a cardboard case covered in satin and lined with silk. France. Around 1880. Lace, mother-of-pearl, metal, weaving, sculpture, gilding. 35 x 67 cm. Acquired from the antique shop at Moskomissiontorg #15. 11490/Pz-369

110 (184). Lace fan with painted silk. Frame with 18 mother-of-

pearl blades. France. Around 1880. Silk, lace, mother-of-pearl, bone, metallic paper, sculpture, weaving, braiding, inlaying. 35.5 x 66 cm. Acquired in 1983 by A. P. Kirillova. 11280/Pz-339

In the centre of the sheet is a young girl seated on a flowering branch, and a gliding Cupid. To the right is found the inscription: Nadine. One the blades a design of garlands of flowers and rocaille scrolls inlaid with metallic paper is indented.

111 (189). Fan: "The Young Girl and the Doves." Frame with 18 mother-of-pearl blades. Painted by Sarita. France. Around 1880. Lace, silk, mother-of-pearl, bone, metal, sculpture, painting, weaving, braiding, inlaying with metallic leaf.

35 x 62 cm. Arrived in 1981 from the Museum of Porcelain in the Kouskovo Château of the 18th century. Coming from the collection of L. I. Rouszkaïa. 11003/Pz-312

The silk insertion at the centre of the lace sheet represents a seated young girl holding a cage in her hand. To the side of her swirl two doves and Cupid. Below is the signature: Sarita. The mother-of-pearl blades are inlaid garlands of gold and silver leaf.

Documentation: Catalogue of the exhibition of 1985, #58.

112 (187). Fan with a sheet of painted silk. Frame with 18 mother-of-pearl blades. Painted by Dailliard. Accompanied by a cardboard case covered in satin. France. Around 1880. Silk, mother-of-pearl, bone, lace,

satin, metal, sculpture, painting, weaving. 32.5 x 61 cm. Arrived in 1984 with national funds of Moskomissiontorg. 11428/Pz-356

The silk sheet represents, in a framing of lace, rose bushes and lilac branches, above which are found two butterflies and a bee. To the right, we see the signature: Dailliard. On the blades motifs of flowers are indented and painted in gold and silver. The interior of the lid of the case carries a ticket: A. Ralley and Co. Kouznetski bridge, Solodovnikov house. Moscow.

113 (190). Fan with a lace sheet. Frame with 18 shell blades. France. Around 1880. Shell, lace, metal, sculpture, melting, weaving. 33.5 x 61 cm. Arrived in 1981 from the Museum of Porcelain at the Kouskovo Château of the 18th century. Coming from the collection of L. I.

Rouzskaïa. 11002/Pz-311

114 (191). Fan: "Flora in a Chariot." Frame with 18 mother-of-pearl blades. Painted by Karo. France. Around 1880. Silk, mother-of-pearl, lace, sculpture, painting. 35.5 x 68 cm. Arrived in 1985 from national funds from Moskomissiontorg. 11547/Pz-395

On the silk sheet, Flora flying in a chariot is drawn, surrounded by five Cupids. Under this representation is the signature: Karo.

115 (192). Fan with two band sheets: "The Rendezvous in the Park." Frame with 16 chiseled mother-of-pearl blades.
Painted by Radou.
France. Around 1890.
Paper, mother-of-pearl, metal, paste, painting, sculpture, gilding.
18.8 x 35 cm.
Acquired in 1986 by E. F. Boulanova.
11624/Pz-412

The sheet is comprised of two

paper bands distinctly painted, fixed together by the blades. On the large upper band, in the centre, is a knight waiting, seated on a park bench. From behind a bush comes a lady who speaks to the knight. At the top on the left is the signature: Anfray. On the lower band, narrower, we see a confused representation of a landscape. Anne-Marie Radou (née Anfray) was a miniaturist painter. (cf.: Benezit, Vol. 8, p. 573).

116 (193). Fan with 18 cellulose blades: "Gallant Scene."
Painted by Jules Donzel.
France. Around 1890.
Paper, cellulose, metal, painting, sculpture.
24 x 45.7 cm.
Acquired in 1986 by L. N. Doudko.
11583/Pz-407

The paper sheet represents a fashionable society composed of six people in a park: three of them are seated on a bench, the others are skipping. The scene is framed with an ornament in rocaille, flowers and baskets containing bouquets. To the left, on the top, is the signature: J. Donzel. In the centre of the blades, we see a basket of flowers painted in silver and gold. The panaches carry quivers of arrows. Jules Donzel was a painter

of the 19th century (cf.: Benezit, Vol. 3, p. 636). He worked in the 1890's at the Kees house and was particularly busy in 1893 (cf.: The Fan. Mirror of the Belle Époque, p. 140-148).

117 (194). Fan with two band sheets: "Gallant Scenes in the Park." Frame with 18 chiseled cellulose blades.
Painted by Jules Donzel.
Accompanied by a cardboard case.
France, Around 1890.
Paper, silk, cellulose, metal, paste, painting, sculpture, weaving.
26.7 x 51 cm.
Acquired in 1986 by V. I. Zametseva.
11564/Pz-401

The sheet of the fan is comprised of two distinctly painted paper bands, held together by the blades. On the upper band, we see three scenes. A little to the left of centre is a knight welcoming a woman, carrying a chair. To the left are a couple of lovers in a park. To the right, a knight on a balcony tosses flowers to a lady holding an umbrella. On the lower sheet, narrower, is drawn a marine landscape with boats and a

waterfall to the right. To the left, in the upper band, is the signature: J. Donzel son. On the back of the right panache, E. Kees is inscribed in gold. The interior of the lid of the case carries the inscription in stamped gold: E. Kees. Maker of Fans. 8 Boulevard des Capucines. Paris.

118 (197). Fan representing a couple feeding pigeons. Frame with 15 mother-of-pearl blades.
Painted by Musoty.
Accompanied by a cardboard case

covered with taffeta (in the style of the 18th century) and lined with red stones.
France. Around 1890.
Silk, mother-of-pearl, sequins, braided lace, painting, sculpture, engraving, embroidery, gilding.
20.5 x 41 cm.
Acquired in 1968 by A. G. Gladkovskaïa.
9659/Pz-265

The sheet represents a seated man and a standing woman feeding pigeons in a park. The painting is framed with an embroidery of sequins, the ornamental motif of which continues onto the blades of the frame. To the right is found the inscription: Musoty. The woven fabric of the interior of the case carries the inscription engraved in gold: Artistic fans. Faucon. 61 passage Panorama. Paris.

Documentation: Catalogue of the exhibition of 1985, #56.

119 (195, 196). Two-sided fan in the style Art Nouveau. Frame with 20 bone blades.
Painted by V.
France. Border between the 19th and 20th centuries.
Paper, bone, metal, painting, sculpture, melting, engraving.
27 x 50.5 cm.
Acquired in 1978 by S. M. Michtchenko.
10819/Pz-274

One side of the sheet represents five female figures in the costume

of the 11th century to the 15th century. Under each of them is a date and an inscription. On the other side is a large half figure of a woman in medieval costume. On each side is a coat of arms. At the bottom on the left we can see the inscription: V. Paris. The design of vegetation engraved on the bone blades is covered in gold.

Documentation: Catalogue of the

GERMANY

120 (200, 201). Two-sided fan: "Gallant Scene in the Park." Frame with 18 chiseled shell blades.
Germany. Around 1840.
Paper, mother-of-pearl, metal, gold and silver leaf, painting, sculpture, inlaying.
28 x 51 cm.
Arrived in 1981 from the Museum of Porcelain in the Kouskovo Château of the 18th century. Coming from the collection of L. I. Rouzskaïa.
11006/Pz-315

One side of the sheet represents a gallant group composed of seven people in a park. The other side, in a medallion, a still-life and two pigeons are presented. On the blades representations of swans, architectural edifices, and landscape motifs are indented.

Documentation: Catalogue of the exhibition of 1985, #59.

ENGLAND

121 (199). Two-sided fan: "Group in a Park." Frame with 16 bone blades.
England (?). 1850-1860.
Bone, paper, bronze, color lithograph, gold stamping, gold and silver painting.
28.5 x 53 cm. Arrived in 1981 from the Museum of Porcelain in the Kouskovo Château of the 18th century. Coming from the collection of L. I. Rouzskaïa.
11007/Pz-316

In a framing of gilded rocaille motifs isa group of nine people in a park, with a young man playing a guitar. On the back, in the centre of the sheet, in a medallion, a servant with a fly-swatter and a servant carrying a crown are represented.

ITALY

122 (202, 203). Marriage fan with two sides. Frame with 14 chiseled mother-of-pear blades.
Italy. 1850-1860.
Paper, mother-of-pearl, painting, sculpture, engraving, gilding.
27.5 x 51 cm.
Acquired in 1979 by P. R. Titova.
10908/Pz-298

One side of the sheet represents a scene in antique style of the dressing of a bride. At the centre, we see the bride, behind which is a servant who holds a necklace. In front of the bride is found the groom kneeling, represented by Hymen. To the right Cupid is presented carrying a crown and a servant bringing out a toiletry case. To the left, near a seated woman, three Cupids braid garlands. On the other side a fashionable society is represented in a park with a fountain. Three ladies in front of a mirror and a knight, a servant and a page offering fruit.

123 (206). Two-sided fan with three cartels. Frame with 14 chiseled bone blades.
Italy. Around 1860.
Paper, bone, metal, silk, amalgamated glass, painting, chromolithography, sculpture, stamping, spinning, weaving, inlaying with silver leaf.
27.5 x 51 cm.
Acquired in 1981 by V. V. Doronine.
11035/Pz-322

One side of the sheet represents, in a framing of complicated designs of vegetation, in three cartels, scenes of a war campaign. On the other side is a bouquet in stamped gold on a silver background. On the panaches small oval mirrors are disposed. In the silk thread and the loop are interlaced metallic cords.

124 (204, 205). Two-sided fan: "Reception at the Doge of Venice." Frame with 16 chiseled mother-of-pearl blades.
Italy. Middle of the 19th century.
Paper, mother-of-pearl, silk thread, painting, sculpture, engraving, gilding, weaving.
27 x 51 cm.
Acquired in 1965 by N. V. Palmtsveig.

9309/Pz-237

The scene represented on the one side of the sheet is inspired by a literary source. In the centre, in front of a throne, on a dais, is a lord in a solemn and accusatory attitude. In front of him, to the right, are two female figures kneeling, a soldier with a lance, a group of men in European costume and four peasants. To the left, we see three dancers, one musician with a lyre, and two young people holding hands. On the other side a genre scene is presented: four young girls with pitchers near a spring.

Documentation: Catalogue of the exhibition of 1985, #53.

SPAIN

125 (208, 210). Two-sided fan: "The Bullfight." Frame with 14 chiseled bone blades.
Accompanied by a red wood case.
Spain. Middle of the 19th century.
Silk, bone, painting, sculpture.
28.5 x 53 cm.
Acquired in 1983 by S. P. Radimov.
11279/Pz-338

One side of the sheet represents a festival with a flamenco dance. On the other side, we see the combat of two matadors and a bull. A vine carrying grapes is represented on the chiseled and openwork blades. The central blades form a badge in

relief, in which is found a basket of flowers.
This fan comes from the collection of the painter P. A. Radimov.

126 (209). Fan: "Gallant Scene with Cupids." Frame with 16 mother-of-pearl blades.
Painted by Gabrielle Eylé.
Accompanied by a cardboard case covered with leather.
Spain. Around 1870.
Skin, mother-of-pearl, painting, sculpture, gilding.

29.5 x 55.5 cm.
Acquired in 1975.
10049/Pz-272

On the left of the skin sheet a group of eight people amusing themselves is represented. A lady holds a fan while seated on the balustrade of a terrace, a couple descend some stairs leading to a body of water. Their figures coincide with the centre of the composition. A boat containing three Cupids moves towards them. To the right, near a fountain, three Cupids frolic. In the left corner is the signature: Gabrielle Eylé. The interior of the case carries a label with the inscription: A. L. "Serra." Cabaliero de Gracia. 15. #5. Carretas. Especialidad en Abanicos artisticos antiquos y modernos. (A. L. "Serra". Cabaliero de Gracia. 15. #5. Carretas. Specialized in artistic, antique and new fans).

WESTERN EUROPE

127 (211). Fan with 22 bone blades executed in the gothic style and decorated with painted embroidery: flowers, geometric figures.
Western Europe. Around 1820.
Bone, silk, sculpture, painting.
17.8 x 35 cm.
Acquired in 1987 by A. A. Grodski. One of the panaches carries an inscription in ink which should not be taken for the date of the creation of the fan: I. 1780.
11698/Pz-430

128 (212, 213). Two-sided fan: "The Pique-Nique." Frame with 14 chiseled mother-of-pearl blades.
Western Europe. Around 1840.
Paper, parchment, mother-of-pearl, sculpture, gilding, silver.
26.8 x 49 cm.
Acquired in 1983 by V. A. Slonimski.
11329/Pz-345

One side of the sheet of parchment represents a pique-nique with six people and a flute player in the middle. On the other side, in the centre of the sheet, a shepherd with two lambs is represented. To the left and right of the central

composition bouquets of flowers are placed.

129 (215, 216). Two-sided fan: "The Concert." Frame with 14 chiseled bone blades.
Western Europe. Middle of the 19th century.
Paper, bone, metal, mother-of-pearl, lithograph, painting, sculpture, awl.
24.2 x 45 cm.
Acquired in 1983 by S. P. Ignatieva.
11330/Pz-346

The two sides of the sheet represent, in the form of chromolithography, groups of musicians. The panaches and the blades can be displaced to the vertical, which permits them to be elongated or shortened. To effect these manipulations, the panaches contain special grooves.

130 (214). Fan: "Gallant Scene in the Park." Frame with 17 bone blades.
Western Europe. Around 1890.
Silk, bone, mother-of-pearl, painting, weaving.
23.5 x 42 cm.
Acquired in 1967 by T. A. Tchoudakova.
9377/Pz-238

The fan is comprised entirely of 17 bone blades, on which is represented a group of four people in a park with a woman playing the flute in the centre.

20TH CENTURY

RUSSIA

131 (217). Fan with 16 openwork bone blades.
Russia. Beginning of the 20th century.
Bone, satin, metal, sculpture, weaving.
19.5 x 32 cm.
Acquired in 1966 by M. N. Kapitanenko.
9375/Pz-236

Documentation: Catalogue of the exhibition of 1985, #67.

132 (219). Lace fan representing

flying Cupids. Frame with 18 wood blades.
Russia. Beginning of the 20th century.
Silk, lace, wood, painting, weaving.
35.5 x 66.5 cm.
Acquired in 1973 by L. M. Kotovskaïa.
10003/Pz-269

Documentation: Catalogue of the exhibition of 1985, #68.

133 (220, 222). Fan in the form of a folding screen. Frame with 17 bone blades.
Accompanied by a case resembling a sheath, covered in blue velvet with a chain in bone and a hook.
Russia. Beginning of the 20th century.
Bone, satin, sculpture, weaving.
28.5 x 29 cm.
Acquired in 1976 by D. A. Barski.
10088/Pz-286

Documentation: Catalogue of the exhibition of 1985, #69.

134 (221). Lace fan. Frame with 18 bone blades.
Russia. Beginning of the 20th century.
Lace, bone, metal, sculpture, engraving, braiding.
24 x 46 cm.
Acquired in 1968 by A. G. Gladkovskaïa.
9656/Pz-262

Documentation: Catalogue of the exhibition of 1985, #70.

135 (224). Black silk lace fan. Frame with 18 black wood blades.
Russia. Beginning of the 20th century.
Silk, lace, wood, braiding, weaving.
35 x 66 cm.
Acquired in 1979 by N. V. Chiriaeva.
10916/Pz-302

Documentation: Catalogue of the exhibition of 1985, #71.

136 (225). Fan in Japanese style representing chrysanthemums. Frame with 15 chiseled cyprus blades.
Russia. Beginning of the 20th century.
Silk, cyprus, cooper, painting,

sculpture, melting.
29 x 55.5 cm.
Acquired in 1980 by E. S.
Barsoukova.
10977/Pz-309

Documentation: Catalogue of the exhibition of 1985, #72.

137 (226). Satin fan embroidered with a representation of flowers and butterflies. Frame with 16 bone blades.
Russia. Beginning of the 20th century.
Satin, lace, silk, bone, chenille, sculpture, embroidery, weaving.
32.7 x 62 cm.
Acquired in 1981 in the antique shop at Moskomissiontorg #15.
11028/Pz-321

Documentation: Catalogue of the exhibition of 1985, #75.

138 (227). Fan with 16 pierced bone blades.
Russia. Beginning of the 20th century.
Bone, silk, sculpture, weaving.
21 x 29 cm.
Acquired in 1973.
11378/Pz-353

The panaches, interlaced with rose garlands in relief, end at the top by, on one side, a ribbon, and the other, by a badge carrying a coat of arms.

Documentation: Catalogue of the exhibition of 1985, #76.

139 (228). Fan with a satin sheet, representing a flowering branch of a wild rose bush. Frame with 16 pierced bone blades.
Russia. Beginning of the 20th century.
Silk, bone, metal, mother-of-pearl, painting, sculpture, weaving.
28.5 x 64 cm.
Acquired in 1984 by S. N. Gousseva.
11390/Pz-349

140 (229). Fan with a black silk sheet representing a wild rose bush, flowers and a bird. Frame with 16 painted wood blades.
Russia. Beginning of the 20th century.
Silk, wood, lace, painting,

sculpture, weaving.
34.5 x 63 cm.
Acquired in 1984 by N. V. Ermolova.
11448/Pz-364

141 (230). Fan with a sheet of goose feathers, painted in Japanese style with flowers and birds. Frame with 28 wood blades.
Russia. Beginning of the 20th century.
Wood, feathers, illumination, sculpture, gilding.
31 x 49 cm.
Acquired in 1985 by E. M. Savonina.
11474/Pz-367

142 (233). Screen fan with 13 shell blades.
Russia. Beginning of the 20th century.
Shell, silk, sculpture, weaving.
25.7 x 19.7 cm.
Acquired in 1985 by C. G. Savtchenko.
11517/Pz-386

143 (232). Fan with a silk sheet representing two flowering branches. Frame with 18 mother-of-pearl blades.
Accompanied by a cardboard case.
Russia. Beginning of the 20th century.
Silk, mother-of-pearl, metal, painting, sculpture, weaving, braiding.
32.2 x 62 cm.
Acquired in 1986 by V. N. Naourits.
11579/Pz-404

The interior of the lid of the case carries a label with the inscription: Moret Store on the Kouznetski bridge in Moscow. At the bottom of the case is another ticket on which is written: 40230. S. Vpe. 1850.

144 (231). Fan with a silk sheet. Frame with 18 pierced bone blades.
Russia. Beginning of the 20th century.
Silk, bone, lace, sequins, metal, painting, sculpture, embroidery.
28 x 42.5 cm.
Acquired in 1986 by E. V. Levchenko.
11581/Pz-405

On the sheet, framed with sequined lace, two doves kissing and flowers are drawn.

145 (234). Fan with 20 pierced and embroidered openwork bone blades.
Russia. Beginning of the 20th century.
Bone, silk, brass, sculpture, weaving.
21.9 x 32 cm.
Coming in 1986 from the national funds of Moskomissiontorg.

11650/Pz-429

146 (235). Fan with a silk sheet painted in the style of "Second Empire." Frame with 16 mother-of-pearl blades.
Russia. 1910's
Mother-of-pearl, silk, sequins, metal, painting, sculpture, weaving.
18.8 x 29.5 cm.
Acquired in 1984 in the antique shop at Moskomissiontorg #15.
11406/Pz-354

147 (236). Fan with a painted silk sheet. Frame with 18 pierced bone blades.
Russia. Around 1910.
Satin, bone, down, painting, sculpture, weaving, appliqué, braiding.
35 x 34 cm.
Acquired in 1986 by A. N. Kartacheva.
11677/Pz-456

On the sheet, framed with down, branches with roses and lilacs and five flying mice are represented.

FRANCE

148 (237). Fan in painted black silk. Frame with 18 bone blades painted in gold.
Painted by Ronot-Tutin.
Accompanied by a cardboard case.
France. Beginning of the 20th century.
Silk, wood, metal, bone, painting, sculpture, gilding.

35.6 x 65.5 cm.
Acquired in 1986 by N. I.
Smirnova.
11580/Pz-406

The sheet represents three birds
on a branch with fruit, surrounded
by thistles and dandelions. Above
the panache is the inscription: R.
T.

Déposé. The bottom of the case
carries the inscription in ink:
Spitzenmalerei. H-25.

149 (239). Fan with a silk sheet
painted in the style Art Nouveau.
Frame with 20 pierced bone
blades.
France. Beginning of the 20th
century.
Wood, silk, metal, mother-of-pearl,
sculpture, painting.
35.5 x 65 cm.
Acquired in 1986 by N. V.
Pigarieva.
11681/Pz-457

The sheet represents irises, small
stones, ducks, flying bees,
dragonflies, and a small bird on a
branch. The painted wood blades
are cut in the form of tree trunks
with leaves and inflorescence in
the upper part. This fan belonged
to the grand-daughter of the poet
F. I. Tioutchev: E. I. Pigarieva (née
Tioutcheva).

150 (240). Fan with a painted
black sheet. Frame with 18
pierced wood blades.
France. Beginning of the 20th
century.
Silk, wood, sequins, metal,
painting, sculpture, embroidery,
weaving, inlaying.
35 x 66 cm.
Acquired in 1985 by V. N. Naourits.
11508/Pz-382

The black silk sheet represents, in
the painting and with the sequins,
a cornucopia, flowers butterflies.
Under the design is the signature:
G. Tutin. The interior of the lid of
the case carries the inscription:
Faucon. Maker of fans. Repairs. 38,

Avenue de l'Opéra. Ancient passage
of the Panoramas. The fan maker
E. Faucon functioned until the
1880's. In the 1890's, the owner of
the factory merged his company
with that of E. Kees. (cf.: The Fan.
Mirror of the Belle Époque, p.
148).

151 (241). Fan with a painted silk
sheet with sequins: "The
Rendezvous." Frame with 18
pierced bone blades.
Accompanied by an imitation
leather cardboard case.
France. Around 1910.
Silk, bone, sequins, metal,
painting, embroidery, sculpture,
engraving, inlaying.
25 x 45 cm.
Acquired in 1982 in the antique
shop at Moskomissiontorg #15.
11200/Pz-333

The pink sheet represents, at the
centre, a scene of a rendezvous in
a park: a knight reclines in front of

a seated woman. To the left and
right of the scene reproduced are
presented partitions and musical
instruments. On the sides, in the
upper parts of the sheet, are
seated ladies in a park. All the
characters are in costume stylized
to the fashions of the 18th century.
The background of the sheet is
decorated in vegetation motifs and
stylized ornamentation, executed
in diverse metallic sequins and two
insertions of transparent gauze.
The blades are inlaid with round
metallic sequins, filled with
designs engraved in painted silver.
A braided ram and a loop of silk
with a chain are suspended from a
hook.

152 (242). Fan representing an
engraving taken from a fashion
journal. Frame with 14 mother-of-
pearl blades.
Duvelleroy House.
Accompanied by a case.
France. 1910-1920.
Silk, mother-of-pearl, feathers,
sequins, engraving on silk,

sculpture, embroidery, inlaying.
20 x 28 cm.
Acquired in 1980 from the antique
shop at Moskomissiontorg #15.
10967/Pz-307

On the sheet a fashion engraving
from the 1820's is printed: two
couples in costumes of the period.
The surface of the sheet is
embroidered with a design of
several figures in steel sequins.
The upper part of the sheet is
framed with a border of down
covered in places with white
mastic. On one of the panaches is
engraved: Duvelleroy. The interior
of the lid of the case carries a
label with the text: Duvelleroy. 17,
Passage des Panoramas and 35
Boulevard des Capucines. Paris.

*Documentation: Catalogue of the
exhibition of 1985, #78.*

SPAIN

153 (243). Screen fan with a
handle case.
Spain. Around 1910.
Wood, fabric, amalgamated glass,
painting, sculpture, weaving,
inlaying.
Length: 35.2 cm.
Acquired in 1983 by L. I.
Vigdorovitch.
11282/Pz-341

The sheet is comprised of two
pieces of fabric, which can fold
into the handle-case of wood,
opening up from inside, and
hollow. From one side, the surface
of the handle-case is set with a
small oval mirror. From the other
side, it is inlaid with the
representation of a small bird and
one can read the inscription:
Ricordo. The sheet extracts itself
from the handle-case and arranges
itself with the help of a silk cord.

NOTES

1) The exhibitions organized from the heart of the museum collection have been able to give a certain impression of the collection of Ostankino. These exhibitions also consisted of fans, which were displayed in the museums of Moscow, of Tver, of Riazan, of Kazan, of Volgorad, of Satatov. At the end of 1983 – beginning of 1984, the exhibition "The Russian Fan of the 18th to the 20th Centuries – Specimens of the Collection of the Palace of Ostankino" was organized in the Russian Museum of Decorative and Popular Art. In 1985-1987, the exhibition hall of the Palace of Ostankino held the exhibition, "The Fans of the 18th to the 20th Centuries – Specimens of the Museum Collection," which was a great success. An exhibition of the same type, which took place at the end of 1988 – beginning of 1989 at the Museum "Château Royal" in Varsovie, and where were shown fans from Ostankino, was no less successful but its composition was a little poorer.

2) "Art of the Serf Artisans of the Palace of Ostankino." Album. Leningrad, 1982. (later: album "Ostankino").

3) Cf. Tcherviakov, A. F., The Commemoration of the Collector: "Decorative Art in the U.S.S.R.", 1966, #8; Museum V. A. Tropinine and the Muscovite Artists of the 19th Century.
Catalogue. Author of the preface and the contents: G. D. Kropivnitskaïa. Moscow, 1975.

4) Cf. Catalogue of the exhibition of fans organized in 1956 at the Palace of Ostankino (private collection of F. E. Vichnevski). Moscow, 1956 (author of the preface and of the contents: N. A. Elizarova).

5) Vassili Cheremetiev. Catalogue of the exhibition. Moscow, 1983.

6) "Decorative Art of the U.S.S.R.", 1967, #4, 1965, #5, 1966, #7; 1967, #1.

7) Ekaterina Vassilievna Goldinger. 80 years of existence. Catalogue of the exhibition. Moscow, 1961.

8) Thus, the exhibition of the National Museum of History counts a little more than 600 fans.

9) Dictionary in 4 volumes of the Russian language. Under the direction of A. P. Evguenieva. Vol. 2, Moscow, 1986, p. 620.

10) Heritage Museum. Catalogue of the fans of the 18th century. Author: S. N. Troïnistki. Prague. Editions Brockhaus-Efron, 1923, p. 7. (later: Troïnitski, already cited, draft).

11) Ibid., p. 8.

12) Ibid., p. 9.

13) Ibid., p. 9.

14) Buss G. Der Fächer. Bielefeld und Leipzig, 1904, p. 26. §. 22 (later: Buss).

15) Thiel E. Geschichte des Kostums, Berlin, 1980, s. 33 (later: Thiel).

16) Troïnitski, already cited, draft, p. 9.

17) Buss. . ., p. 58, §30-31. Blondel S. History of Fans. . . Paris, 1875, p. 72. (later: Blondel...)

18) Archipiscopate Véniamine. New table of the law or explication of the church, of the liturgy and of all religious services and sacred objects. St. Petersburg, 1899, p. 199-200.

19) Baro C. M. and Escoda J. Ancient Fans. Lausanne, 1957, p. 5. (later: Baro-Escoda...) Blondel..., p.58, 61. Fan accompanied by its case, having belonged to the Queen Théodelinde de Lombardie. The object was most likely made famous by its publication by the architect William Woorg in 1875 (Mayor S. Collecting fans, Kingston, 1980, p.7).

20) The Art of Composition and Painting of the Fan, the Screen, the Paravent. By Fraipont. Paris, p. 135. (later: Fraipont...)

21) Fraipont... ,p. 135. "The Fan" by Octave Uzanne. Paris, 1882, p. 43. (later: Uzanne...).

22) From the word "fly."

23) Cf. Troïnitski, already cited, p. 10; Baro-Escoda... , p. 5; Blondel... , p. 61.

24) Uzanne... , p. 42; Baro-Escoda... , p. 6; Troïnitski. Already cited, p. 11, and others.

25) Troïnitski. Already cited, p. 11; Mazé-Sencier A. The Book of the Collectors. Paris, 1885, p. 773. (later: Mazé-Sencier...) ; Vermeersch G. Fan. In "The Ancient Art at the National Belgian Exhibition." Brussels – Paris, 1882, p. 325.

26) Thiel E... , p. 199.

27) Buss... , p. 104, §. 61.

28) Thiel E... , p. 219.

29) Buss... , p. 219.
Italian fan of the middle of the 16th century in the form of a flag in fabric with a staff in wood. Conserved at the National Museum of Bavaria (Cf. Fächer. Kunst und Mode aus fünf Jahrhunderten. Aus den Sammlungen des Bayerischen Nationalsmueums und des Müchner Stadtsmuseums. München, 1987. Kat. 1, t-50).

30) Verechtchaguine V. The Fan and Grace – Ed. "Starye gody." 1910, April, p. 19. (later: Verechtchaguine. The Fan and Grace,...).

31) Uzanne... , p. 79. Blondel... , p. 141.

32) Verechtchaguine. The Fan and Grace. Troïnitski. Already cited.

33) Case (Cf. Sawaitov P. I. Description of old Russian vases, costume, armament, armors and horse armors. St. Petersburg, 1896, p. 120; later: Sawaitov. Already cited, p...).

34) Zabeline I. E. The Costumes of the Russian Czars from the 16th to the 17th Centuries. 1st part. Moscow, 1896, p. 273. (later: Zabeline. Already cited,).

35) Zabeline. Already cited. Part 2, Moscow, 1915, p. 63-66.

36) Zaozerski A. I.. The Field-Marshal B. P. Cheremetiev. Moscow, 1989, p. 15-16.

37) Zabeline. Already cited. Part 1, p. 700.

38) Mazé-Sencier... , p. 779-780.

39) The Antiques of the Russian State, published on the order of the Emperor. Part #5, Moscow, 1853, p. 103.

40) Ibid., p. 104.

41) Viktorov A. Description of the Accounts and the Old Orders of the Court. 1584-1613. 1st edition. Moscow, 1877. p. 30-31.

42) The Antiques of the Russian State... , p. 104.

43) Ibid., p. 103.

44) Year 138. May 29, the clerks Gavrilo Oblezov and Boulgak Molovanov brought back to the palace of the sovereign Czar and His Highness Michel Feodorovitch of all of Russia, a screen with a handle of very green jasper, mounted on gold; the jasper is worth 5 roubles; the gold, 6 roubles. A white jasper ornament is inlaid with gold; in the middle of the screen, in a gilded blade, is a ruby, of a value of 8 roubles. And on the other side of the screen, in the middle of a blade, a ruby with a value of 3 roubles; in two blades are 20 ruby stones, each of which has a value of 1 rouble, and two sapphires of a value of 2 roubles, 34 ruby fragments; each fragment is worth ten kopecks. And the whole of the screen is valued at 56 roubles and 10 kopecks. And the sovereign Czar of all of Russia, His Highness Michel Feodorovitch, offered it to his son, His Highness very knowing, the CzarevitchAlexis Mikhaïlovitch, and the CzarevitchAlexis Mikhaïlovitch placed the screen in his treasury. (Zabeline, already cited, Part 1, p. 701).

45) Zabeline. Already cited. Part 1, p. 706.

46) Troïnitski. Already cited, p. 13.

47) Swaitov. Already cited, p. 100.
Fabric worked and undulated in thick silk with silver and gold netting (ibid., p. 87).

48) Oukhanova I. N. The Sculpture of Bone in Russia in the 18th to the 19th Centuries. Leningrad, 1981, p. 16-18 (later: Oukhanova. The Sculpture of Bone in Russia, p...). Zabeline. Already cited. Part 1, p. 270-271.

49) Zabeline. Already cited. Part 1, p. 273.

50) Ibid., p. 273.

51) Ibid., p. 712. Type of small sapphire (Sawaitov, already cited, p. 70).

52) Ibid., p. 727.

53) "Subsequently, when gallantry instituted in our societies certain conveniences, the following entered into morals: During dances, the master of the house would bring a bouquet of flowers to a lady who he would like to honor. This lady would be the queen of the dance, ordering the dances and giving the bouquet solemnly to another cavalier, in designating the day when she would desire to dance at his house. The cavalier who received the flowers was obliged to blindly bend to the will of the belle. On the day before the indicated day, he would send her a fan, a pair of gloves, as well as flowers, with which she would appear in public, and as long as she was the possessor of the bouquet, she would remain the queen of the dance until the next election." (Russian Morals Under Peter I – Ed. "Rousskaïa." Pocketbook for the amateurs of the fatherland in 1825. Part 1, St. Petersburg, edition A Kornilovitch, 1824, p. 105-106); Chtcherbatov M. M. The Degradation of Morals in Russia Ed. "Rousskaïa." Vol. 2, St. Petersburg, 1870, p. 39.

54) Oukhanova. The Sculpture of Bone in Russia, p. 170-172.

55) Verechtchaguine. The Fan and Grace, p. 30. Troïnitski, already cited, p. 18-19.

56) Verechtchaguine. The Fan and Grace, p. 31.

57) Ibid., p. 31.

58) Troïnitski. Already cited, p. 24.

59) Chinese emblems and symbols, transposed in Russian, Italian, French, German and English, first in Amsterdam, and now in St. Petersburg, printed, reproduced and corrected by Nestor Maximovitch Ambodik. St. Petersburg, 1788, p. XXIX, XXXIV, XXXV (later: Emblems and Symbols...).

60) Starikova L. M. New Documents Concerning the Activity of an Italian Troupe in Russia in the 30's of the 18th Century and the Amateur Russian Theater of the Period; in the book "Monuments of the Culture. New Discoveries. 1988." Moscow, 1989, p. 86.

61) Troïnitski. Already cited, p. 12.

62) "The Bulletin of St. Petersburg." 1799, #30, 15 April, p. 704.

63) "The Bulletin of Moscow." 1798, #80, 10 November, p. 1729

64) Ibid., 1797, #22, 18 March, p. 472.

65) Ibid., 1797, #22, 23 March, p. 595.

66) Ibid., 1797, #37, 9 May, p. 815.

67) Ibid., 1797, #49, 20 June, p. 1053.

68) Troïnitski. Already cited, p. 14.

69) "The Bulletin of St. Petersburg." 1796, #40, 16 May, p. 895.

70) Ibid., 1797, #38, 12 May, p. 731.

71) Ibid., 1799, #47, 14 June, p. 1135.

72) "The Bulletin of Moscow." 1791, #71, 6 September, p. 1391.

73) Ibid., 1795, #60, 28 June, p. 1215.

74) Ibid., 1796, #57, 16 July, p. 1093.

75) CGADA (National Archives) form. 277, inv. 2, d. 1734, 1752-1753, I. 1. T. T. Korchanova mentions this same manufacturer in his book "Costume in Russia from the 18th to the Beginning of the 20th Century – Collection of The Hermitage Museum." Leningrad, 1979, p. 12. But given that the family name of the owner was badly recorded, it is designated under the name of "factory of Vladimir Roujnov."

76) Ibid.

77) Ibid., I. 5.

78) Ibid., I. 12.

79) Ibid., I. 5.

80) Ibid., I. 9.

81) Ibid., I. 5.

82) Ibid., d. 1735, 1754-1759, I. 2.

83) Ibid., I. 12-13.

84) Ibid., d. 1736, 1757, I. 1-2.

85) Ibid., I. 3.

86) Ibid., d. 1738, 1765-1768, I. 1-9.

87) Ibid., d. 1738, 1765-1768, I. 1-9.

88) Ibid., I. 7.

89) Diderot M. and d'Alembert M. Encyclopedia or Reasoned Dictionary of the Sciences, The Arts and the Trades. Collection Book of Plates on the Sciences and the Arts. Paris, 1765. Vol. III. Fan makers, pl. I-IV (later: Diderot M. and d'Alembert M. ... Collection Book of Plates... , pl...)

90) Oukhanova. The Sculpture of Bone in Russia, p. 172.

91) CGADA (National Archives) form. 397, inv. 1, d. 1761, I. 8.

92) Complete Collection of Laws. St. Petersburg, 1830. Vol. 22, I 123, p. 370-371.

93) Oukhanova. The Sculpture of Bone in Russia, p. 174.

94) The Great Soviet Encyclopedia. Vol. I. 1929, p. 798.

95) The Bible. Genesis. Chapter 24. St. Petersburg, 1900, p. 24-26.

96) The Bible. First Book of Kings. Chapter 25, p. 96-98.

97) Nemilova I. S. The Hermitage Museum. French Painting. 18th Century. Catalogue. #59, p. 108-109.

98) The opera completa di Guido Reni. Presentazione di Cesare Garboli. Milan, 1971. Tav. XX-XXI. Cat. 72. The favorite subject of the famous fresco of Guido Reni was visibly reproduced more than one time on the fans of the 18th century. We see it, for example, on one of the French fans of the Spanish collection (cf. the catalogue "Fans of Spain." Joachima Baio. Madrid. 1920. Tabl XXIII). Suzanne Mayor expresses the same idea. She confirms that in the painting of fans of the 18th century, in Italy as in other countries, among the classic subjects, the fresco of Guido Reni titled "Aurora" was very often used (cf. Mayor S. Collecting Fans, p. 29).

99) Broussilovitch D. Persianova O., Roummel E. Motifs, Mythologies, Literature and History in Painting, Sculpture and Tapestries of The Hermitage. Leningrad – Moscow, 1966, p. 19-20.

100) Inv. #3120/G-40.

101) Mazé-Sencier... , p. 748.

102) Troïnitski. Already cited. p. 24-26, tabl. 21,24.

103) Emblems and Symbols... , #433, p. 111.

104) Ibid., #120, p. 30.

105) Ibid., p. 48.

106) Ibid., #241, p. 62.

107) Diderot M. and d'Alembert M. ... Collection Book of Plates... , pl. I-IV.

108) Felkerzam A. Ivory and Its Application in Art. Ed. "Starye Gody." 1915, October, p. 14.

109) Verechtchaguine. The Fan and Grace, p. 36. Troïnitski. Already cited, p. 25. Tabl. 23.

110) Mazé-Sencier... , p. 778.

111) Ibid.

112) Baro-Escoda... , p. 9.

113) Fraipont... , p. 142.

114) Thus, in his book "Art Nouveau: Sources, History, Problems." Moscow, 1989, D. V. Sarabianov speaks of a coexistence, at the beginning, of baroque and classic procedures.

115) Troïnitski. Already cited, p. 13.

116) Baro-Escoda... , p. 7.

117) "The Satirical Journal", Part 4, Moscow, 1790, p. 23.

118) Pokrovski V. "Elegance in the Satirical Literature of the 18th Century." Moscow, 1903, p. 43 (later: Pokrovski. Already cited).

119) Ibid., p. 43.

120) "The Fan of a Belle is the Scepter of the World." Epigraph taken from Uzanne...

121) Baro-Escoda... , p. 7. Translated by the author, A. F. Tcherviakov.

122) Uzanne... , p. 104. Translated by the author, A. F. Tcherviakov.

123) Work of Derjavine. St. Petersburg, edition D. P. Chtoukina, 1845, p. 181; Dmitriev I. I. Works. Moscow, 1986, p. 136-137.

124) Pokrovski. Already cited, p. 43.

125) Pokrovski. Already cited, p. 103.

126) Pyliaev M. I. Old Moscow. St. Petersburg, 1891, p. 5.

127) The Journal of the Voyage of B. N. Zinoview to Germany, Italy, France and England. 1784-1788. Ed. "Rousskaïa." Vol. 23, 1878, #10, p. 232.

128) "The Satirical Journal", p. 24-25.

129) Troïnitski. Already cited, p. 11.

130) Oukhanova I. N. The Russian Lacquer Ware in The Hermitage Collection. Leningrad, 1964, p. 9, ill. 10-11.

131) Buss... , p. 110 §. 73.

132) "Year 1802. The . . . May. Inventory effected in the village of Ostankovo, at the city hall, with a gallery and a theater possessing diverse pieces of furniture and ornaments." Service of Written Sources of the Museum of Ostankino. Inv. # 10855/PI-2997, I. 101 and 89.

133) Service of Written Sources, inv. 1802, I. 101.

134) Service of Written Sources, inv. 1802, I. 89.

135) Uzanne... , p. 103. Blondel... , p. 166.

136) Iakounina L. I . The shawls created by the serfs. Beginning of the 19th century. "Work of the National Museum of History." Edition XIII. Moscow, 1941, p. 233-250.

137) Uzanne... , p. 121.

138) Verechtchaguine V. A. Souvenirs of the Past. Articles and Remarks. St. Petersburg, 1914, p. 61 (later: Verechtchaguine. Souvenirs of the Past).

139) Oukhanova. Sculpture of Bone in Russia, p. 178.

140) Ibid., p. 104-105.

141) Oukhanova I. The bone sculptures coming from Kholmogore to St. Petersburg from the 18th to the beginning of the 19th centuries. "Information of The Hermitage Museum." XV, 1959, p. 15-17.

142) Fraipont... , p. 142. Verechtchaguine. Souvenirs of the Past, p. 61.

143) "The Sun of Russia", 1913, #11, p. 3.

144) Dike C. Systematic Canes. A Fabulous and Unknown World. Paris-Geneva. ill. 40. Blondel... , p. 179.

145) Kibalova L., Guerbenova O., Lamorova M., Illustrated Encyclopedia of Fashion. Prague, 1988, ill. 804.

146) The Fan. Mirror of the Belle Époque. Museum of Fashion and Costume. Paris, 1985, p. 14.

147) "The World of Fashion." Illustrated journal for women. St. Petersburg, 1877, #13, April 1st, p. 131.

148) "The Moscow Bulletin", 1872, #244, 30/IX.

149) "The Bulletin of St. Petersburg", 1869, # 280, 17/X and # 283, 14/X.

150) Annual of Kiev for the year 1905. Kiev, 1905, p. 33.

151) "The Moscow Bulletin", 1872, #292, 19/XI.

152) Oukhanova. Sculpture of Bone in Russia, p. 178.

153) Uzanne... , p. 126. Blondel... , p. 173.

154) Thus, in St. Petersburg at the beginning of the 20th century, Alexandre possessed warehouses, workshops and a store on the Nevski Perspective at #11. ("All Russia", Russian annual of the fabricators, factories, industries of commerce and administration of 1912. Moscow, 1912, p. 3728).

155) Mazé-Sencier... , p. 738-784.

156) Great Encyclopedia. Reasoned Inventory of the Sciences, Letters and the Arts by the Society of Scholars and People of Letters. Vol. 16, p. 885.

157) "The Bulletin of St. Petersburg", 1872, #116, 11/V.

158) The Moret Store in Moscow (Petrovka, 10) was then bought by M. Bourdon. (account book of A. P. Bakhrouchine "Who Collects What?". Moscow, 1916, p. 67-68). The workshops, the warehouses, and the stores of Ralley and Company were situated in Moscow as well as in St. Petersburg ("All Russia", 1912, p. 2511-2512).

159) "The Moscow Bulletin", 1872, #16, 19 January.

160) D. V. Sarabianov created a general study dedicated to Art Nouveau ("Art Nouveau. Sources, History, Problems").

161) Kiritchenko E. I Russian Architecture from 1830 to 1910. Moscow, 1979, p. 204-209.

162) The Duvelleroy house, which produced the best fans in the world, was created in 1827 by Jean-Pierre Duvelleroy. It was handed down to his son in 1887 and, passing from hand to hand, it continued to exist until 1981. Its work was begun again in 1983. (cf. "The Fan. Mirror of the Belle Époque", p. 146).

163) Buss... , p. 66-69, 130, §. 32-35, 108.

164) Vrangel N. N. The Blood and the Fan. Ed. "Starye gody." 1915, October, p. 41.

165) Among the Russian model painters at the beginning of the 20th century, some (like S. Tchekhounne) turned their attention toward the theme of the fan. They integrated fans into assortments of costumes (cf. Strijenova T. K. : "The History of Soviet Costume." Moscow, 1972, p. 56). The interest in fans has not weakened abroad. In recent years, several countries, in particular Spain, have witnessed a veritable "boom" of fans. This is reflected, for example, in the journal "Izvestia" from August 30, 1988.

BIBLIOGRAPHY

Verechtchaguine V. The Fan and Grace. Ed. "Starye gody",
1910, April.

Verechtchaguine V. Souvenirs of the Past. Articles and
Remarks. St. Petersburg, 1914.

Viktorov A. Description of Accounts and Documents of the
Old Ordinances of the Palace. 1584-1613. 1st edition.
Moscow, 1877.

The Antiques of the Russian State, published under the
orders of His Majesty. Part V, Moscow, 1853.

Catalogue of the exhibition of fans organized at the Palace of
Ostankino in 1956 (from the private collection of F. E.
Vichnevski). Moscow, 1956. (Author of the preface and the
contents: N. A. Elizarova).

Zabeline I. E. The Morals and the Costumes of the Russian
Czars in the 16th to the 18th Centuries. Part I, Moscow,
1895.

Korchounova T. T. Russian Costume from the 18th to the
Beginning of the 20th Centuries. Collection of The Hermitage
Museum, Leningrad, 1979.

Pokrovski V. Elegance in the Satirical Literature of the 18th
Century. Moscow, 1903.

"The Satirical journal, a journal permitting the deriding of
the wrinkled foreheads of old people, the purchase of which
can amuse and instruct young ladies, young girls, dandies,
scatterbrains, young dandies, players and people in another
situation, written in an imaginary year, in a month unknown,
on a date ignored, by an unknown author." Parts 1-6, Moscow,
1790.

Heritage Museum. Catalogue of the Fans of the 18th Century.
Author: S. N. Troïnitski, Prague, Editions Brockhaus-Efron,
1923.

Oukhanova I. N. The Sculpting of Bone in Russia in the 18th
to the 19th Centuries. Leningrad, 1981.

Tcherviakov A. F. The Fans of the 18th Century, Album "The
Palace of Ostankino – Museum of the Art of the Serf Artisans
of the 18th Century." Leningrad, 1982.

Exhibition: "The Fans of the 18th Century – 20th Century.
Collection of the Palace of Ostankino – Museum of the Art of
the Serf Artisans of the 18th Century." Catalogue. Moscow,
1985. (Author of the preface and the contents: A. F.

Tcherviakov).

Baro C. M. and Escoda J. Ancient Fans. Lausanne, 1957.

Blondel S. Intimate Art and Taste in France. (Grammar of Curiosity). Paris, 1884.

Buss G. Der Fächer. Bielefeld und Leipzig, 1904.

Champier V., Knab L. Fan – In "The Great Encyclopedia. Vol. 16. Reasoned Inventory of the Sciences, the Arts and the Trades." Paris.

Diderot M. and d'Alembert M. Encyclopedia or Reasoned Dictionary of the Sciences, the Arts and the Trades. Collection Book of Plates on the Sciences and the Arts. Paris, 1765. Vol. III. Fan Makers, pl. I-IV.

The Fan, Mirror of the Belle Époque. Museum of Fashion and Costume. Paris, 1985.

Exhibition of "El Abanico en Espana." Cataloguo general ilustrado por Joaquin Ezquerra del Bayo. Madrid, 1920.

Fächer. Kunst und Mode aus fünf Jahrhunderten. Aus den Sammlungen des Bayerischen Nationalmuseums und des Münchner Stadtmuseums. Müchen, 1987.

Fraipont G. The Art of Composition and Painting of the Fan, the Screen and the Folding Screen. Paris.

Illustrierte Geschichte des Kunstgewerbes. I-II b. Berlin. Kybalova L., Hervenova O., Lamarovaz M. Das grosse Bilderlexikon der Mode. Dresden, 1980.

Mayor S. Collecting Fans. Kingston, 1980.

Mazé-Sencier A. The Book of Collectors. Paris, 1885.

Müller-Krumbach R. Alte Fächer. Weimar, 1985.

Rhead. History of the Fan. London, 1909.

Thiel E. Geschiche des Kostums. Berlin, 1980.

Gustave Uzanne, "The Fan." Paris, 1882.

Vermeersch G. Fan. In "The Ancient Art of the National Belgian Exhibition." Brussels-Paris, 1882.

Zakrzevska E. Czarkowska I. Fans 18th – 19th Century. National Museum. Warsaw.